W9-BSN-552

MEETING COMMON CORE TECHNOLOGY STANDARDS

Strategies for Grades 3-5

Ela Area Public Library District
275 Mohawk Trail, Lake Zurich, IL 60047
(847) 438-3433
www.eapl.org

31241008714993

JUN - - 2016

Valerie Morrison | Stephanie Novak | Tim Vanderwerff

International Society for Technology in Education
EUGENE, OREGON • ARLINGTON, VA

Meeting Common Core Technology Standards
Strategies for Grades 3-5
Valerie Morrison, Stephanie Novak, and Tim Vanderwerff

© 2016 International Society for Technology in Education

World rights reserved. No part of this book may be reproduced or transmitted in any form or by any means—electronic, mechanical, photocopying, recording, or by any information storage or retrieval system—without prior written permission from the publisher. Contact Permissions Editor: permissions@iste.org; fax: 1.541.302.3780.

Editor: Paul Wurster
Associate Editor: Emily Reed
Production Manager: Christine Longmuir
Copy Editors: Jennifer Weaver-Neist, Kristin Landon
Cover Design: Brianne Beigh
Book Design and Production: Jeff Puda

Library of Congress Cataloging-in-Publication Data available

First Edition
ISBN: 978-1-56484-369-2 (paperback)
Ebook version available

Printed in the United States of America

ISTE® is a registered trademark of the International Society for Technology in Education.

About ISTE

The International Society for Technology in Education (ISTE) is the premier non-profit organization serving educators and education leaders committed to empowering connected learners in a connected world. ISTE serves more than 100,000 education stakeholders throughout the world.

ISTE's innovative offerings include the ISTE Conference & Expo, one of the biggest, most comprehensive ed tech events in the world—as well as the widely adopted ISTE Standards for learning, teaching and leading in the digital age and a robust suite of professional learning resources, including webinars, online courses, consulting services for schools and districts, books, and peer-reviewed journals and publications. Visit iste.org to learn more.

Contents

About the Authors

VALERIE MORRISON graduated with an elementary education degree from Northern Illinois University (NIU) and began her career as a classroom teacher. She became interested in teaching with technology early on and was a computer teacher for two years at a K–8 private school. Morrison then switched to the public school system, where she obtained a master's degree in instructional technology with an emphasis in media literacy from NIU. She gained 14 years of experience as a technology director / technology integration specialist and technology coach. Morrison worked closely with teachers and students to plan and differentiate lessons and projects that integrate technology. She taught technology workshops and classes for teachers and oversaw the technology program at her school. (She loves working with kids, teachers, and technology!) Like her coauthor Tim Vanderwerff, Morrison regularly served on her district's technology committee, and was involved with integrating current state and district standards with the latest educational technologies. She presented at various conferences, including a presentation in Springfield, Illinois, to state legislators, where she and coauthor Stephanie Novak briefed legislators on how schools use technology. Morrison has recently switched career paths and is now teaching education classes at the college level; she enjoys using technology to teach the next generation of teachers. She also has time to write now, which allows her to further educate the current generation of teachers.

STEPHANIE NOVAK knew from a very young age that teaching and working with kids was the right career path for her. She graduated from Northern Illinois University with a master's degree in reading and earned a reading specialist certificate from National Louis University. Novak started teaching at the middle school level but eventually settled in the elementary school system. As a classroom teacher for 27 years and an extended-learning teacher and coach for the past seven years, she has always felt learning should be fun and meaningful. Novak was on her school district's technology committee for many years and regularly tried new technology in her classroom. As an instructional coach, she encouraged teachers to help students grow in their learning at a pace that allows for the most intellectual and personal growth. For the past two years, Novak guided Grade 1–5 teachers through the Common Core State Standards, teaching them how to blend these standards with rigorous curriculum and prepare students for the digital age. After many years in education, Novak recently retired. She now looks forward to applying her years of experience in a consulting capacity for administrators, teachers, and students. She also plans to continue to publish stories that describe her successful experiences in the field of education.

TIM VANDERWERFF has an extensive background in teaching and technology that began in the '70s. Although writing this book was a new experience, trying out new experiences in education are second nature to him. After graduating from Illinois State University and then earning a master's in educational administration from Northern Illinois University, Vanderwerff saw many federal and state initiatives come and go in his 33 years of teaching. Starting as a classroom teacher in Grades 2–5, he was on his school district's technology committee for many years and regularly tried new technology in his class during that time. Vanderwerff eventually moved to the library media center at his elementary school in 1987. He was the librarian and the technology teacher, and he provided tech support for the building for many years. In 2010, he was asked to be a teaching coach, which involved sitting in on grade-level team meetings, finding resources for the new Common Core State Standards, supporting individual teachers and teams in the classroom (both with technology and with the newest educational strategies), and advising new teachers. Vanderwerff is recently retired, allowing him to devote more time to writing about the field in which he is so passionate.

DEDICATIONS

For Team Media, without whom we could not have done what we did!
    –Valerie Morrison

To Bill; all my family; my confidant, Kim; and my District 96 friends.
    –Stephanie Novak

To my family: Kim, Eric, Michael and Kristina.
    –Tim Vanderwerff

Acknowledgments

We are grateful for the contributions of our friends, teammates, colleagues, and assistants with whom we worked throughout the years and who helped us come up with ideas for our first four books—this series. Working with so many talented people, we appreciate the collaboration and teamwork that allowed us to learn a great deal about coaching and technology. We would especially like to thank Linda Litvan and June Fox for their contributions to the "Practical Ideas" chapters in this book (Grades 3-5).

We would also like to thank our families for all of their amazing support during the writing of this series. During the many times we spent meeting, editing, and struggling to write, their unwavering support was truly appreciated.

Also, we would like to thank the editors and their staff at ISTE for their insight, guidance, and patience. Their ongoing support has been much appreciated as we've gotten familiar with the process of publishing.

Introduction

Have you ever found yourself sitting in a meeting wondering, "How am I ever going to change all my lessons to fit the new Common Core State Standards?" At that moment, you also realize your district wants you to integrate the latest digital-age technology, and that has you asking yourself, "Where will I get this technology? Will it be provided for me, or am I responsible for purchasing and providing the technology?"

All of this might seem overwhelming—what is a teacher to do? First, you might turn to your teammates and colleagues for help and support. Perhaps your district provides current technology development for staff on a regular basis and has instructional coaches to help teachers chart this new territory, planning new lessons, bringing in resources, and infusing technology. In reality, most districts don't have all of this support. Yet teachers are especially in need of technology when considering their clientele: students.

Until recently, every state was doing their own thing when it came to standards. The Common Core State Standards (CCSS) is a U.S. education initiative seeking to bring diverse state curricula into alignment with each other by following the principles of standards-based education reform. The CCSS is sponsored by the National Governors Association Center for Best Practices (NGA Center) and the Council of Chief

State School Officers (CCSSO), and a vast majority of the 50 U.S. states are members of the initiative. So, if you are in a Common Core state, there are big changes happening. Even if you're in a state that's not adopting Common Core, there is a high likelihood your curriculum will soon look very similar to the CCSS initiative.

We, as coaches, have an important role in helping you, the teachers, and your students during this transition. Our hope is that you are in a district that provides high-quality professional learning experiences regularly to help teachers understand the shift from existing sta te standards to the CCSS. Professional development, along with this book and its resources, will help you identify the changes you will need to make to guide your instruction using CCSS with technology and help support you in transferring new knowledge and skills to the classroom. It is a large task, but focusing on specific goals for student learning utilizing the CCSS with technology will have a positive effect on student achievement. And it will build your capacity as a teacher.

CCSS were designed to prepare K–12 students for college and career success in the areas of English language arts, math, science, and social studies. CCSS defines the knowledge and skills students should have in their K–12 education, with an emphasis on learning goals as well as end-of-year expectations.

Most states have had English language arts and math standards in place for a few years. However, these standards vary, not only in coverage but also in levels of rigor. CCSS is very explicit about what is expected of students at each grade level. Students, parents, teachers, and school administrators can now work together toward common goals. CCSS will be consistent from school to school among states choosing to adopt the standards. If students or teachers transfer to different schools, they will all be assured that learning expectations will be the same. Any student, no matter where they live within a Common Core state, can be assured that they will be able to graduate from high school, get ready for college, and have a successful career.

The standards first launched in June 2009. State leaders from the CCSSO and NGA developed them together with parents, teachers, school administrators, and experts from across the country. Both national and international research and evidence informed development of the standards. After public comment, organizers released the final version of the CCSS in June 2010.

The CCSS were written in a clear, understandable, and consistent manner to align with college and work expectations. These standards contain rigorous content, as well as an application of knowledge through higher-order skills. CCSS are evidence based, and they build on the strengths and lessons of current state standards.

Writers of CCSS also gathered information and advice from top-performing coun-tries to ensure that U.S. students are prepared to succeed in a global economy and society. Here is a helpful link from the Common Core State Standards Initiative's **"About the Standards"** page: **(http://tinyurl.com/26f7amp)**.

Transition to the Common Core will be a challenging task for your students as well as for you. With the implementation of these new standards, students will be expected to become self-directed and critical readers, writers, and thinkers. At the same time, you will need to make adjustments. In fact, you will need to shift your entire instructional practice.

Shifting your instructional practice will require a great deal of work and commit-ment, but this will all be well worth the effort for both you and your students. By breaking things down into small steps, the transition will seem less overwhelming.

This book is part of a collection of four books designed to help teachers connect technology to the Common Core in their classrooms. We learned how to do this by teaching together, and we have more than 85 years of combined teaching experi-ence. As teammates, we worked with students, teachers, and administrators to integrate technology in the same school district. Our hope is that you will think of this book as your coach, because we can't be with you personally. We hope to show you how to integrate the newly embedded tech-related language found within the standards into your everyday curriculum.

In Chapter 1, we address some of the issues that your students face and discuss how important it is to tailor their learning experiences. Today's students are the first generation to truly grow up in the age of the internet, complete with emailing, texting, instant messaging, social networking, tweeting, and blogging. Teaching this new generation of children, teenagers, and young adults can be challenging because of how digital technology has affected their brains and behaviors. The Common Core curriculum has kept this new generation of students in mind, and so will we.

In Chapter 2, we explore the importance of engaging and educating parents. We fol-low this up with a discussion in Chapter 3 about the equipment you need to teach the standards, and we show you how to address the roadblocks that stand between you and this technology. There are always roadblocks that educators commonly face, and we hope to show you how to get around them effectively so that you—and your students—can succeed. We should also mention that although we are sharing many tools and resources with you, we are not affiliated with any company. The programs, apps, and websites listed in this book are simply those that we feel sup-port the standards.

In Chapter 4, we discuss effective staff development, and we explain in Chapter 5 how the CCSS is organized. Chapter 6 takes a deeper look at the specific standards for the grade level you teach. With these standards in mind, we show you how to begin, offering several classroom-tested lesson ideas in Chapters 7–10 that will ensure your students are satisfying the tech-related benchmarks outlined in the CCSS.

We realize that technology is constantly changing and that digital tools come and go. To make certain that you continue to have the most current resources at your fingertips, visit **our website (http://tinyurl.com/oexfhcv)**. The website password for the 3-5 book is: 35MCCTS. There, you will find an updated list of the apps, software, and websites mentioned in this book.

Let's begin by taking a closer look at today's generation of tech-savvy students and the skills they bring to the classroom.

Chapter 1

Today's Students

A two-year-old taking a selfie? Seven-year-olds tweeting? No doubt about it, today's students come to school knowing more technology than ever before. New educational research suggests that offering a variety of learning opportunities, including lots of technology options, may be the best way to engage today's generation of learners. Educators need to respond to this generation and address their unique learning needs. We, the authors, believe this so passionately that we think a chapter about this subject is a must in any book about teaching children in the digital age. Technology must be made more available and at students' fingertips. Technology must become ubiquitous.

The CCSS are designed to bring school systems into the digital age. They are designed with the tech-savvy child in mind. Actually, the standards are designed with their future workplace in mind. That is the driving force behind the technology we see in the standards and why teaching to your students' future needs is extremely important. Please keep this mind as you read this chapter.

Who Are Your Students?

The students you now have in your classroom grew up using digital technology and mass media. According to Debra Szybinski, executive director at New York University's Faculty Resource Network, (http://tinyurl.com/pqwr7va), this generation is:

> ...a generation characterized by some as self-absorbed, attention-deficit-disordered, digital addicts who disrespect authority and assume that they can control what, when, and how they learn, and by others as smart, self-assured, technology wizards, who follow the rules, and who are on their way to becoming the powerhouse generation. Clearly, this is a generation like no other, and that has posed an entirely new set of challenges both in and out of the classroom for faculty members and administrators alike.

Some of you are part of this younger generation. If so, you were the first to truly grow up in the age of the internet: emailing, texting, instant messaging, and social networking. Yet the current generation is ever changing. Those born even 15 years ago did not have technology so pervasive that it was with them 24/7. Many students entering school now are completely immersed in technology outside of school.

Ironically, at many schools, there is a disconnect to students' real lives and their way of learning. Schools are often islands of 20th-century thinking in a 21st-century world. Schools must do a better job of reaching the current generation of students; they need to respond to and address students' unique learning needs. Technology needs to be constantly available to students at school.

What Does This Generation Know and Do?

Many children entering kindergarten now have access to desktop computers, smartphones, tablets, and/or laptops at home. These children begin using all or most of these devices by the time they are three years old. Whether you go to playgroups, parks, or wherever, you're likely to see young children who are working on their parents' tablets or smartphones (or begging to use them!). These students come to us with skills that include (but are not limited to) swiping to work an app; navigating a mouse to play computer games; operating their own electronic devices, such as children's learning tablets, handheld learning devices, and interactive video games; and hunting and pecking on the keyboard to send emails. Also, our tech-savvy students can take videos and photos using a tablet or smartphone, as well as converse with someone by texting, blogging, and messaging. Most have been exposed to the internet and understand that they can find almost any kind of information there.

Because they have so much information at the touch of a button and constant stimulation around them, this generation is often attempting to multitask. It makes sense to them to watch TV, send a text, and find out what the weather will be all at the same time!

Some say that the current generation has hovering parents and a sense of entitlement. While this may be taken as a negative, having parents who are involved with their children and their children's school is a good thing, as it strengthens the home–school connection. Students who have parents who are involved in their academic life can be better students, and they are less afraid to try new things. We, as educators, need to recognize these traits and use them to help students reach their maximum potential.

Being social is very important to the students in this tech-savvy generation. They are certainly the "in touch" generation, with immediate access to texts, emails, social networking sites, and even the sound of a human voice at the other end of the line. This generation is lost when their smartphone or tablet breaks down; they feel "cut off from the world" when they don't have instant access to the internet.

How Has Technology Affected Students' Minds?

By the time they're in their 20s, today's students will have spent thousands of hours surfing the internet and playing video games. This vast amount of screen time seems to be shortening their attention spans. At a time when their brains are particularly sensitive to outside influences, excessive screen time affects the way they learn and absorb information.

Furthermore, this generation does not read books to find information. Online search engines are prevalent in providing all of the information they need quickly, without having to go through a book from cover to cover. With access to an overabundance of information, they need to be skilled hunters who know how to sift through data quickly and efficiently. This new learner doesn't necessarily read from left to right or from beginning to end. Visuals help today's students absorb more information than they do from straight text. Thus, students become better scanners, a useful skill when confronted with masses of online information in a world that's full of noise and multiple stimulations. So, most modern students have learned to block out distractions while they focus on the task at hand.

How Has Technology Affected Behavior?

Because of the constant use of technology, there is less and less face-to-face communication taking place. We all have seen instances of parents and children sitting next to each other without speaking at a restaurant. Instead, they simply sit and quietly engage with their individual tablets or smartphones.

There are many debates about how technology helps or harms the development of a student's thinking. Of course, this depends on what specific technology is used, as well as how and with what frequency it is used in school. Our duty as educators is to decide what technology to use in the classroom and when, because technology influences students' thought processes. We educators need be aware of this effect to guide our students in becoming 21st-century learners.

How Do We Move Beyond the ABCs?

Education has gone through a monumental transformation in the last 20 years. Some changes have greatly improved the way teachers educate, while others are still under evaluation. The great debate between play-based preschool versus learning-based preschool is a case in point. What we have found during our years as teachers is that to progress in the classroom, teachers have to adapt to the times, adopting new techniques while continuing to use time-tested methods. Success in teaching a new generation of students isn't based solely on what we are teaching them but, rather, how we are teaching them.

We have seen our share of success stories and our share of students who have struggled for reasons that are completely preventable when these students have the right tools. For these highly activity-scheduled and gadget-oriented students, traditional one-size-fits-all teaching is no longer effective. Sitting behind a desk, listening to the teacher talk, and reading from a textbook are completely ineffective. This generation of students needs to be engaged in active and interactive learning to enhance their knowledge. They do not want technology just because it is "cool." They need technology because it drives their world now and will continue to drive their world in the future. They are looking for something dynamic, to make learning come alive—to make it different and interesting every day. Being connected accomplishes that goal.

How Can Educators Succeed in the Digital Age?

Thinking that technology is a new toy that will go away or doesn't have a place in education is no longer an option. We need to embrace technology and tap into what our students are already coming to us with, using it to advance their learning. But this technology cannot just be digital worksheets!

This is not always easy, especially when students know more about how to use the technology than many teachers. Therefore, it is our duty to catch up and make sure we know what our students know. This can be done in many different ways; however, the easiest way is to do what they do: pick up tablets or smartphones and start playing with them! Once we have the background skills to know what our students know, we can move forward. We simply need to remember that technology is a tool. And we can use these tools like anything else we use in education—manipulatives in math, novels in reading, and microscopes in science, just to name a few.

Of course, this new reality being imposed on and by the current generation has implications for you as a teacher. It used to be that students conducted research by using books that were from credible publishers, and those books went through rigorous editing and fact checking. This generation uses the internet almost exclusively. If your students get all of their information from the internet, then you must teach them media literacy skills. This skill set has become extremely important in an information age where children need to discern fiction from fact on the internet when, sometimes, we adults have trouble differentiating it for ourselves.

You need to tap into what your students are experiencing every day and use it to your advantage. Many of your current students will work in very social settings but in a different way than previous generations. Let them work often as partners or in groups to create multimedia presentations or digital videos. Because they love to send emails and video chat, let them email, instant message, or video chat with students around the world! This generation is good at multitasking. Allow them to do more things at once, such as opening multiple screens while taking notes on a research paper. Students all know how to use a smartphone, so when on a field trip, let them record a video of what they are seeing. They are used to constant noise and stimulation. Do not make them work quietly at their desks; rather, they should work with hands-on activities like live apps or green-screen technology. Students know at a very young age how to navigate the internet. Let them run to the computer when they have a question instead of asking you for the answer.

We know this new generation of children, teenagers, and young adults can be challenging because of how digital technology has changed their way of learning and behaviors. The following chapters will further address some of these issues and how learning needs to be specialized, giving more examples of how to integrate technology with the new CCSS. The Common Core curriculum has kept this new generation of students in mind, and so will we.

Chapter 2

Parent Education

The past decade has been financially difficult for schools. States across the country have had to slash education budgets because of downturns in the economy. If your district's budget was not affected by financial cuts, it is among the few. As for the rest of us, we have had to achieve more with less. To make matters even more challenging, we now have new standards that ask schools to immerse students in technology—a very expensive task. Having parents on your side in this budget struggle can be very helpful.

In the years since the CCSS were written and adopted by most states, some attitudes toward the standards have changed. More recently, parents and community members have begun to question them. So it is important, as a teacher, to be proactive in getting the word out about what is going on in your classroom. Work with parents and the community to educate them about CCSS in your state, district, and school. Parents only want what is best for their children, and a little reassurance from you can go a long way.

This reassurance begins with listening to parents. Ask them about their concerns. Answering their questions with facts will help them to better understand why your state adopted the standards.

The following are just a few of the technology concerns that have been raised about the CCSS recently. Knowing about them and other controversial issues allows you to defuse concerns before they become major issues.

Why Do Parents Need to Know about Technology Standards?

You don't need technology to read and you don't need technology to do math–civilizations have been doing both for centuries. Nevertheless, you must admit that technology does help in both areas. If we were still at the turn of the last millennium (1000 AD), we would be hand-copying books. The printing press brought books to the commoner and education to those who wanted to learn. The abacus is fine but hardly as good as a calculator or a computer. Technology marches on so that we can advance, learn more, and pass that knowledge along to the next generation.

The computer revolution of the last century is finally hitting the classroom with the encouragement of the CCSS. Before these standards, the pervasive use of computers was for schools with money or those who could write winning grants. Even so, many schools that were thought to be advanced had not integrated technology into everyday learning. The Common Core is the first set of widely recognized standards to do that. But why do parents need to know about them? There are several reasons.

First, keeping students versed in the fundamentals of technology will enhance your teaching tremendously, and students' parents can help with this at home. Survey parents to see if they have internet access and broadband at home. What kind of equipment do they use–do they have cameras or video capabilities? What do they allow their children to use? Knowing what your students have or do not have at home evens the playing field in the classroom. Encourage parents to teach their children how to use tablets, computers, video cameras, and other mobile devices so students come more prepared to school.

Second, learning doesn't just happen at school. You need to educate parents because they are the main support system for learning away from school. Consistent, clear standards now put forward by CCSS enable more effective learning. Knowing what technology and what software will be used to master these standards greatly assists parents and, in turn, their children. Look at the **Harvard Family Involvement Network of Educators** website **(FINE, http://tinyurl.com/hguh777)** for the latest research and insights on how to get students' parents involved.

Third, technology can instantly link parents to what their children are learning. Knowing assignments, communicating with teachers, and understanding what is expected are all improved with today's technology. There is even an article out there (DeWitt, 2013) about a principal who tried "flipping" parent communication, which you might try too. Whatever you implement is a win-win for you and your students. Take advantage of technology in communication; don't shun it. It will make your life easier.

Finally, we are becoming a smaller, more codependent world. To have a world-class education that keeps our nation and civilization moving forward, all students need to be well versed in the newest technology. That is what the CCSS are all about! The Common Core State Standards Initiative's mission statement affirms, "The standards are designed to be robust and relevant to the real world, reflecting the knowledge and skills that our young people need for success in college and careers" (Council of Chief State School Officers & National Governors Association Center for Best Practices, 2010). In other words, the CCSS is designed for your students' success as adults in the work world, where technology is integral.

Even so, parents must be a part of this endeavor or their children will still struggle to succeed. Involving them is as important to you, as a teacher, as is any other aspect of your students' learning. Do not think of parent education in the CCSS as an add-on—a tool to be used if you have time. Investing in your students' parents and having them on your team benefits you and lessens your load. In a synthesis of studies done on families, communities, and schools, Henderson and Mapp (2002) stated, "Efforts to improve children's performance in school are much more effective if they encompass their families. Regardless of income level or education background, all families can—and often do—support their children's success." (p. 208)

What Issues Do Parents Have with Technology in CCSS?

Parents may ask you about some of the controversial things they are hearing in the news related to the Common Core. One controversy involves a misunderstanding about standards and curriculum. Standards describe what students should know; curriculum is how they get there. For example, even though there is no standard for cursive writing or keyboarding, that doesn't mean it won't be in your school's curriculum. Curriculum is still developed locally. Educate parents who are concerned that they have no control over their child's curriculum—they still have the ability to contribute to what is taught in their local school.

Another controversy centers on test scores from states that adopted CCSS early on: scores decreased. Although it may or may not be true in your district, scores quite often decrease when the format of the tests changes. One example is when students go from paper-and-pencil tests to digital assessments. According to Swanson (2013), if your school changed tests, then a result might be decreased scores until students become familiar with the new format. The best way to combat this is to have other digital tests in the classroom throughout the year, to make your students feel more comfortable with the new format.

A common concern we have heard as teachers and as CCSS coaches is that the federal government will be able to collect the data of individual students because of these digital tests. This has been a particularly heightened apprehension recently. The fact is, there are laws passed by the U.S. Congress (2010) that prohibit the creation of a federal database with students' personally identifiable information. Although the law is in place, you should still be vigilant about keeping this sensitive data secure. You are the first line of defense and need to have procedures in place. Please go over your district's student privacy policy. If there is none, push hard to make one.

How Can Parents Help with Assessment Technology?

As the teacher, you should help parents and community members understand the types of questions and problems that students are asked to solve on the new digital assessments. During parent nights, open houses, and/or in newsletters, introduce parents to the **Partnership for Assessment of Readiness for College and Careers (PARCC, www.parcconline.org)** and **Smarter Balanced Assessment Consortium (www. smarterbalanced.org)** websites. You can download sample questions to show to parents; and it can also be helpful to put new assessment questions next to old assessment questions so everyone can directly observe the shift.

If your state is going to use the Smarter Balanced test, have parents use the sample questions at the PARCC site to test their children at home. The sample Smarter Balanced test can also be used to prepare for the PARCC test. Both tests' questions are similar and based on the CCSS.

Don't forget the basics. Make sure parents know what kind of equipment the students will be tested on, and have them use similar equipment at home if possible. This will make the device a secondary concern so your students can focus on the test. And send home a sample question weekly so parents can become familiar with the changing assessments. Make sure some of the sample test questions you send home require students to use technology to answer the question, as this will be included on the assessments.

How Can Parents Help Students Meet Technology Standards?

Parents need to see the value of having technologies at home that can help their children achieve more. At the same time, home technology will help you accomplish these new curriculum tasks that, as we teachers know, are daunting, to say the least.

A recent poll by the Leading Education by Advancing Digital (LEAD) Commission (2012, p. 23) found that parents and teachers believe students who lack home access to the internet are at a significant disadvantage. Home access to broadband is viewed as important to learning and doing well in school for the following reasons.

- Home access greatly exceeds anything that your students could ever bring home in their backpacks.

- Home access allows parents to become more involved in their child's school-work and allows more effective communication between parent and school, thus promoting greater student success.

- Having home access vastly expands the time your students can learn and explore.

- Home access leads to greater collaborative work, engaging students in online group homework. (This last point dovetails perfectly with many of the new CCSS technology initiatives).

Home access needs to have your active support. At the beginning of the year, run a workshop for parents about the kinds of technology you will be using and why. Teach them how to monitor their children for internet safety as well. You may want to call on your library media specialist or tech specialist to help you if they are available in your school.

Of course, you may teach in an area where parents do not have the funds to have broadband access or technology at home. Following are a few ways to address the issue.

- For homes that have broadband but no computers/tablets, start a program that allows students to check out resources from the school overnight.

- Have after-school clubs or homework help where technology is available.

- Open the school in the evenings for parents and students, providing them access to teachers and to the technology they need.

- Apply for one of many grants available from different levels of government, foundations, and companies to help with your school community's access to technology.

Wherever you teach, parent education is the key to student success with the state standards. Lack of information is one of the main reasons parents are opposed to the CCSS. Being a proactive partner with them will defuse most objections that arise—from parents and from others in the community—and actually create proponents of what is going on in your classroom through this challenging time. Having parents as partners can only help when you are faced with technology needs, such as lack of hardware and software, lack of assistance, and gaps in your students' tech knowledge.

Parent education is only part of the puzzle, however. You must first educate yourself about the CCSS and technology before you can effectively educate anyone. To address this, we have included a chapter on staff development (Chapter 4). But before we explore your professional development options, let's take a closer look at the roadblocks you may encounter on your journey to get technology into your classroom.

Chapter 3

Roadblocks to Technology

U nless your school or district has unlimited funding and gives you completely free reign on your purchases, you have hit roadblocks in your quest for classroom technology. Chances are that you do not have the student technology to become a fully stocked digital age learning environment, but you are not alone. In this chapter, we provide ideas to best use and manage the equipment and software/apps you do have, and we explore ways to get more. It is our hope that when we come to the later chapters on practical ways to integrate your technology into the new Common Core curriculum, you will be better prepared to maximize your resources.

What Are the Roadblocks to Accessibility?

If it is not possible to provide all of your students with tablets or laptops, providing half the class access to this technology is the next best thing. This allows you to work with small groups or pairs of students. Another option is to share technology with the classroom next door to gain at least some time with a full class set of laptops or tablets.

Lack of funding for 10–12 Tablets/Laptops per Classroom

One option is to have each grade level share a cart of 15 laptops or tablets in addition to a roving cart that any classroom can access. We would suggest grade-level sharing of technology with no more than three sections, as more sections limit student use further. If there are four or more sections in a grade, more carts should be added. This will allow the grade level to have access to at least half a class set. When you need a full class set, use the mobile cart to fill in the gaps. Another way to share additional mobile devices is to divide the 15 laptops or tablets into sets of five for each of three classrooms and then have teachers share devices if a class needs more. You could also place all 15 laptops or tablets on a cart and provide a signup sheet for as-needed use.

Only 4–6 Laptops/Tablets per Classroom

You can use four to six laptops or tablets as a learning center or have half the class double up on them at one time. You can also share with other classrooms near you to get more. You could do this by picking a time every day when two or three classrooms share their laptops or tablets for an allotted amount of time; you could have certain days when you each have them; or you could ask for them informally. The key is easy accessibility.

Computer Lab Limitations

A computer lab with enough computers for all of your students is another great resource, especially if it includes a tech or media center teacher or assistant. This is great because everything is in a set location and there is another knowledgeable teacher available to help. The negative is that you have to sign up for certain times, and everyone must work on the computers at the same time. If you have access to tables in the lab or in a nearby learning space, however, you have the opportunity to do other things with students who have finished their work on the computer, forming small work groups as you would in a traditional classroom.

Additional Equipment

How do you choose additional technology to better equip your classroom when your budget is already tight or inadequate? Aside from laptops and tablets, it is imperative to have a multimedia projector so that all students can see lesson materials, projects, resources, etc. Other equipment that is valuable to includes:

- **Document cameras:** You will use these every day to display written books, worksheets, student work, and the like. Once you have one, you won't know how you got along without one!

- **Interactive whiteboards:** These are great for engaging students, especially during whole-group instruction.

- **Color printer:** Access to a color printer makes student work come to life. (Younger students especially love color!)

- **Scanner:** Access to a scanner will help when you wish to scan documents or pictures and allows for immediate replication of student's work.

We could have included interactive response systems as well; however, with so many new websites available that can turn your laptops, tablets, or smartphones into interactive technology, buying response systems is no longer necessary.

Some interactive websites that are free (and may offer an upgrade for an affordable fee) are:

- **Socrative (www.socrative.com)**

- **Exit Ticket (http://exitticket.org)**

- **Annotate (https://annotate.net)**

Keeping Up with Students' State Assessments

Different groups developed PARCC and Smarter Balanced to test for college and career readiness starting from Grade 3 onward. Your students may be tested three or four times a year. PARCC and Smarter Balanced (with very few exceptions) are the two main tests that states use to provide teachers the information they need to help students become successful with the Common Core standards. These two assessments are computerized and also have certain technology requirements, but they allow traditional paper-and-pencil versions when necessary. (Teachers should still be aware that traditional versions may be phased out eventually.)

We will not address the specifics of network requirements; just know that your school or district will need to meet certain operating system and networking specifications whether they are using the Smarter Balanced or the PARCC assessment. Additionally, your network must be able to address security requirements to keep student information safe. Following are informational sites to help you find what you will need.

- **PARCC technical requirements: (http://tinyurl.com/jmhyrey)**

- **Smarter Balanced technical requirements: (http://tinyurl.com/nuaqy6u)**

How Do We Overcome Software and Hardware Roadblocks?

You cannot benefit from technology if you don't have it. It is also difficult to share it if you don't have enough of it. You need it on time and easily accessible if you truly want to use it seamlessly. This may be the biggest roadblock. We discussed above how you can use different configurations of new or existing hardware in your school. The more pervasive the technology, the easier it will be for you to achieve the goals set forth by the Common Core.

Sources of Funding

If you don't have enough equipment and/or software, you can apply for grants. While there are more grants available for economically disadvantaged districts, some are accessible to all districts. State and federal grants are available, for example, especially if you can link your needs to the Common Core. The Bill & Melinda Gates Foundation and big companies like Google, Target, and Staples give to schools. Ask your PTA/PTO for money. Many districts have foundations that grant teachers money. You could even ask the PTA/PTO to do a fundraiser for new technology. Following is a list that is by no means complete but offers a great place to start.

GOVERNMENT

- **21st Century Community Learning Centers (http://tinyurl.com/7nx37vb):** This funding is designed to get parents and the community to actively support your work in the classroom.

- **Individuals with Disabilities Education Act (IDEA, (http://tinyurl.com/77b2dwa)**: These funds are for students with disabilities.

- **Grants.gov (http://tinyurl.com/k8fybkt):** Search this site for all available federal grants. These grants include:

  - Investing in Innovation Fund (i3)

  - Race to the Top Fund: The government provides grants for Race to the Top specifically for the CCSS.

  - Title I, Part A—Improving Basic Programs Operated by Local Educational Agencies

  - Title I, Section 1003(g)—School Improvement Grants (SIG)

- Title I—Supplemental Education Services (SES)

- Title I, Part C—Migrant Education

- Title I, Part D—Prevention and Intervention Programs for Children and Youth Who Are Neglected, Delinquent, or At Risk

- Title II—Professional Development

- Title II, Part D—Enhancing Education Through Technology (EETT)

- Title III—English Language Acquisition State Grants

- Title VII, Part A—Indian Education

- **Computers for Learning (http://computersforlearning.gov):** This government program encourages agencies to transfer their used computers and related peripheral equipment directly to schools.

- **State Government (http://tinyurl.com/oexfhcv):** Look for your state's educational website in this online index.

FOUNDATIONS

- **Bill & Melinda Gates Foundation (http://tinyurl.com/odwcrra):** This is the largest, private foundation in the world. Its primary aim in the U.S. is to expand educational opportunities and access to information technology.

- **The Foundation Center (http://foundationcenter.org):** This independent, non-profit, information clearinghouse collects information on foundations, corporate giving, and related subjects.

- **Foundations.org (http://tinyurl.com/7sf3c):** This online resource provides an A–Z directory of foundations and grant makers.

- **The NEA Foundation (http://tinyurl.com/or2qc56):** This teacher association gives grants in several areas.

COMPANIES

Many of the companies that manufacture the products we use every day have educational initiatives that offer grants for public schools. Following are just a few.

- **Target (http://tinyurl.com/cdt25kz):** Target offers grants in many areas, including: education, the arts, and public safety.

- **Toshiba (www.toshiba.com/taf/k5.jsp):** Toshiba also offers math and science grants for Grades K–5.

- **Google (http://tinyurl.com/pm9gar4):** Google has several sites dedicated to corporate giving. Google for Nonprofits is a good place to start your search.

- **Microsoft Corporate Citizenship (http://tinyurl.com/p62et7u):** These grants are available for after-school programs.

- **Staples Foundation (www.staplesfoundation.org):** Staples Foundation for Learning teaches, trains and inspires people from around the world by providing educational and job skill opportunities.

- **CenturyLink Clarke M. Williams Foundation's Teachers & Technology Program (http://tinyurl.com/otej8rl):** These grants are designed to help fund projects that advance student success through the innovative use of technology. Teachers in public or private PK–12 schools in CenturyLink's residential service areas are eligible to apply for a Teachers and Technology grant.

OTHER RESOURCES
- **National Charter School Resource Center (http://tinyurl.com/ph2ytng):** This resource website has many links to funding opportunities.

- **eSchool News (www.eschoolnews.com):** This is a great grant resource for K–12 and higher education.

- **Internet@Schools (http://tinyurl.com/nnh5n9d):** This online magazine for education provides a vast list of free resources, grants, and funding.

- **Scholastic (http://tinyurl.com/nd3t97t):** This educational mainstay has many great grant resources too.

Free Software and Apps

Software and app purchases are a challenging roadblock, especially if your district or school doesn't provide enough funding. Fortunately, there are many free resources. Search app stores and type in "free." Free sites, such as Google Docs, are also great places to start. In addition, there are entire sites with free services geared toward the CCSS.

If you are in a small district or a private school, or if you live in a state where funding is limited, follow the money. Go to websites in states and at schools that do have the funds. Look at websites in wealthier school districts near you. Do they have CCSS lessons, activities, and technology ideas that are free to anyone on the internet?

Many states have CCSS resources posted for free! Take advantage of them. For example, New York has many helpful suggestions at **engageNY.org (www.engageny. org/common-core-curriculum)**. Utah has also published a very resourceful Common Core site, which can be found at the **Utah Education Network (UEN, http://tinyurl. com/l2e532).**

Free software and apps are also available from private companies. These sites usually have ads, or they may want you to purchase add-ons; you and your district will have to judge their value for yourselves. More examples of free applications and websites will be given in the "Practical Ideas" chapters of this book.

What Other Roadblocks Must We Solve?

Systemic educational roadblocks can take many forms, which are often unintended or unavoidable. Here are three common challenges teachers face.

Misguided Policies

Some districts or schools require that all classrooms have the same apps or software. They don't allow teachers to choose what they prefer, and this can be frustrating. If your district wants all software to be the same, you might try explaining why each grade level and each teacher would benefit from using different software, apps, and equipment appropriate to their students' needs.

Some districts implement policies that do not allow teachers to use technology as a tool. Instead, they force teachers to use technology when other mediums or tools make more sense. For example, we discovered a district that required teachers to teach with a tablet 85% of their instructional time. This district even required students to bring tablets to gym class and physical education teachers to use tablets in every class period. School leaders who enforce this kind of policy know very little about infusing technology into the classroom. It would be better to achieve higher technology use through staff development and individual coaching (for example, through the use of this book) than by generating untenable policies that don't actually affect meaningful student learning.

To counter these policies, speak to your principal, go to a technology meeting, or attend a board meeting! Explain that technology is a tool and that the CCSS does not expect you to use technology every second of the day. There is a time and place for technology just as there is a time and place for math manipulatives, a calculator, a book, and even a pencil. Balance is the key. If anything is overused, it (and your effort) is set up for failure.

Parents

Parents will ask the question, "Why do we need new technology?" Have a discussion at PTA/PTO meetings, open house nights, and board meetings about what you will be doing or would like to do with technology. Explain that the CCSS expects everyone to integrate technology, and this is important for our today's students. Please refer to the chapter on parent education (Chapter 2), which has specific suggestions about many of the issues that become parental roadblocks.

Staff Development

Teacher training is so important. You need to have professional development in the area of technology for yourself as well as for your students. If you have a technology coach, great! Spend a lot of time with this coach—set up weekly meetings. They can help you as well as model or coteach with you. There are many professional development opportunities online as well as off-site in the area of technology. Refer to Chapter 4 to learn how to get staff development outside your district and how to best get around these roadblocks!

How Do You Get the Help You Need?

One of the key components of using technology is getting help. It is very difficult to manage a class of young students who are all trying to use technology at the same time. This is also the case when teachers try to work with a small group while the rest of the class is doing something else on tablets. Inevitably, something goes wrong with someone's computer or students are not sure what to click next. You can teach them to use a few apps or programs if you do it consistently, especially in a self-contained classroom center where students are engaged in independent and self-directed learning activities. However, when you want to expose them to something new or want to change the routine in any way, it is extremely helpful to have another set of hands.

Most elementary classrooms are not fortunate enough to have a full-time aide with them. Therefore, you will need to get more creative. If you have assistants who come to you on a regular basis to help in the classroom, this is a great resource. You can schedule technology use for when they are in the room. This allows greater freedom to work with the whole class—assuming you have enough equipment. You can teach while your assistant goes around the room problem solving. If you work in small groups or at a media center, you each can take a group, doubling your efforts.

If you do not have access to assistants, you might try using parent volunteers. The worst part of using volunteers is inconsistent attendance. However, if you can find a parent or two who is willing to come in on a regular basis, they can be a great help. You will need to find time to train your volunteers, of course, but once you do, most will be savvy enough to pick up what they need to do in class.

If you don't have access to assistants or volunteers, training students is an option. When you are working with a group, have tech-savvy students problem solve technical issues. When you are setting up, they can go around and help other students prepare. We have successfully had student experts as young as first grade. Four or five students can be used to go around the room to help with small tasks, such as printing or finding an app. Training them is fairly easy too. You can do so at recess or during one of their free periods, and it is helpful to have a checklist for them that outlines what you want them to learn. Following are examples of what to put on your checklist.

- How to save

- How to print

- How to find and open software

- How to open apps

- How to carefully handle the equipment

- How to charge devices

- How to distribute equipment (usage policies)

- How to check internet connectivity

- How to use search engines

Make sure that you post passwords where it is easy for students to find them. Forgotten passwords are an annoying occurrence, so having them easily accessible for all will help you manage the situation comfortably.

Another option is to work with your fellow teachers. Consider arranging your schedules so that you each take extra students while the other uses technology with a smaller group. Overseeing fewer students makes technology use much easier to manage.

Create peer groups that have a mix of tech-savvy students and those who struggle with technology. Arrange a time when older students can work with your younger students. Older students like to work with younger ones, and older students can be a big help in classroom management. Making the most of available technology is all in the management.

Although there can be many roadblocks that prohibit you from using classroom technology the way that you would like, there are ways to overcome these challenges. By using the suggestions given in this chapter, we hope you will overcome any roadblocks that lie in your way and that you have most everything you need at your fingertips.

Chapter 4

Staff Development

When technology integration is at its best, a child or a teacher doesn't stop
to think that he or she is using a technology tool—it is second nature. And
students are often more actively engaged in projects when technology tools
are a seamless part of the learning process.

—"What Is Successful Technology Integration?" (Edutopia, 2007)

Without a doubt, today's student comes to school with a strong background
and understanding of technology. This generation of tech-savvy students
is interested, motivated, and even driven by technology. As you will see, CCSS has
explicit technology standards within grade levels. But technology, as a tool, needs
to be infused in all other CCSS standards as well. Having a tech-savvy classroom for
today's students is the best way to create a digital age learning environment.

Truly integrated technology is ever present but invisible. You can use technology
as a tool for instruction—as a way to vary the way you present information. You can
also provide technology options for students as a way for them to engage in content
skills. And students in your class should be given opportunities to create and share
their new learning with a myriad of technology tools. The CCSS are not just about
presenting information to students; today's students need to be able to plan, reason,

analyze, evaluate, and create. Technology integration in today's classroom will do just that—it will not only allow your students to become more engaged in the learning process but empower them to gain a deeper understanding of their learning.

A plethora of articles have been written about the success of CCSS and how good professional development for teachers and staff is a significant key to its success. Technology plays a very valuable role in guiding and fostering this effective professional development, as well as helping to boost current professional-development resources and practices. And technologies that make tools available to teachers on an ongoing basis present a solid jumping-off point for successful classroom integration.

Research has found that sending teachers to workshop-based professional development alone is not very effective. Approximately, 90–100% of teachers participate in workshop-style or in-service training sessions during a school year and through the summer. While workshops can be informational and timely, teachers need opportunities to implement new teaching techniques, not just learn about them. Thus, professional development needs to be ongoing and meaningful to your own professional circumstances. The most effective professional development also uses peer coaches and mentors to implement new learning in class.

How Do You Create a Technology Plan?

You need lots of support and tools to utilize and sustain technology in your classroom. If you do not have a district or school technology director or coach, how do you develop a plan to get yourself (as well as your fellow colleagues) what is needed? You can be the pioneer to get the technology ball rolling.

Following are suggestions to help you begin the journey of infusing technology in your classroom. Although this should not be your task alone, sometimes it falls to a single individual to blaze the trail. Fortunately, there are many online resources that can assist you with creating a technology plan. **Edutopia** is a well-known place to start, offering (among other things) "Ten Steps to Effective Technology Staff Development" **(http://tinyurl.com/oesjsmn)**.

The first step is to put together a technology committee with as many representatives from different buildings and grade levels as you can find. It would be great to include administration staff, as well as a district office representative. Parents, students, and outside technology experts can only enhance your committee.

Next, come up with some ways to show how you and your students can use technology in the classroom. Providing specific examples of students working with technology to address the ISTE Standards and the CCSS would be powerful!

Develop a detailed questionnaire for teachers to express their classroom needs, frustrations, and fears. This questionnaire can also serve as a place for teachers to describe what they hope to learn from professional development, including technology goals they would like students to pursue in class.

Ask students to describe the ideal state of technology in their classroom. Ask them how they envision the state of technology in their classroom in one year, two years, five years, and so on. Then place the ideas from this brainstorming session in a public document so everyone on the committee and in the community can see and refer to it.

Lastly, conduct a teacher survey using the **ISTE Standards for Teachers** as a guide **(www.iste.org/standards)**. These standards outline what teachers should know and be able to apply in order to teach effectively and grow professionally. ISTE has organized them into the following five categories:

1. Facilitate and inspire student learning and creativity

2. Design and develop digital-age learning experiences and assessments

3. Model digital-age work and learning

4. Promote and model digital citizenship and responsibility

5. Engage in professional growth and leadership

Each standard has four performance indicators that provide specific, measurable outcomes. You can use them to ascertain teachers' technology comfort level, attitude, and integration use in your school. Answers could be on a scale, such as "proficient enough to teach someone else," "able to hold my own," "a little knowledge," or "scared to death to even try." It may even be helpful to have teachers identify three to five areas that they feel are most important to improving technology within the year. Providing a space for them to write an explanation is also important, as they may not be able to rank themselves on a scale when they can't quantify what they don't know. Writing a paragraph about where they stand with technology might be easier for them. The data you gain from this survey should be shared with your building, other participating schools, the administration, and the district office. And you may want to consider repeating this comfort-level survey several times throughout the year.

Once you've determined the proficiency of staff members, you can enlist their help to create a digital folder of suggested lesson plans, activities, and projects for all to access and use. Your colleagues will not only be able to implement the folder's learning opportunities in their classrooms but add to the folder as they try new things. Something you may want to consider having is a reflection page to accompany any lesson, activity, or project posted. This will help others learn from and refine the ideas as they implement them on their own.

Additionally, your meetings, questionnaires, and survey results will identify teachers, staff members, parents, and administrators who have expertise in specific technology areas. Talk to your principal or district administrators to see if funding is available to pay for the planning time and workshop your experts may wish to lead. (As a rule of thumb, for every hour of professional-development class time, it takes at least two hours of planning.) Opportunities also need to be offered to your experts to advance their professional development. Perhaps you can even find a way to tap into the technology expertise of students, parents, and/or community members by having them lead some of your professional-development workshops. If possible, build in this professional development/collaboration time at least once a week. Carrying on conversations about the workshops at team meetings, staff meetings, even lunch is a great way to foster and gain interest in what you and your committee are doing.

Even if you are not willing or able to head up a technology committee, there are many things you can do to prepare your classroom for digital-age learning.

What Are Some Staff-Development Ideas?

Be creative in your pursuit of ongoing staff development. If you are pressed for time, observe other teachers who use technology in their classrooms. (Ask your principal, department head, or coach to find someone to cover your classroom so you can do this.) If you are fortunate enough to have a coach or staff-development person in your building or district, ask them to set up a weekly meeting with you to work on technology goals. If you do not have a coach, partner up with another teacher or two. Peer coaching, team teaching, peer modeling, or even just conferring with other teachers is a great way to advance your goals, objectives, and outcomes.

There are many conferences and workshops offered throughout the year. Check to see if your district will cover the expense and provide substitutes so you and your colleagues can attend. Check out the Bureau of Education & Research (BER, www.ber.org). They are a sponsor of staff-development training for professional educators in the United States and Canada, offering many technology workshops and seminars about how to implement technology with the Common Core. There are also many technology grants offered by businesses. The magazines **Innovation & Tech Today (http://innotechtoday.com)** and **Tech & Learning (www.techlearning.com)** are good places to look for these opportunities.

Ask your principal to provide grade-level time for teachers to look at standards and plan how technology can be used. Then, as a group, develop activities, projects, and lessons that include technology; come up with management strategies for using technology; and (perhaps most important) decide how you are going to assess and evaluate students' learning. This team time is so important for you to brainstorm, share and develop ideas, and gather materials. Summer is also a good time for you and your colleagues to get together to collaborate and develop projects. Check with your district to see if they will provide paid time for your summer work.

Don't forget to share your own successes and those of others. Share disappointments as well so that others can learn from them. Take pictures, write press releases, post on your school's website, and include what you are doing in your parent newsletters and emails. If possible, make a short presentation at a school board meeting. Who knows? You may gain the moral and financial support you're looking for! Share your successes any way you can.

Because needs continually change, keep planning and re-evaluating where you are and where you want to be. Encourage teachers to reach for the stars with their technology needs. Ask students how they feel about using technology and how it has affected their learning. These suggestions will help you and your colleagues get the technology you need.

Where Can You Learn about Staff Development?

There are a multitude of professional-development opportunities out there for technology, either in the workshop/conference format or online (accessible from the comfort of your home or classroom). Some opportunities are free, and some come with a membership fee to use the website or attend organization events. Others are priced per event. Following are a few suggestions.

- **ISTE (www.iste.org)** has several fantastic staff-development resources, including its Professional Learning Networks (PLNs), which allow you to instantly connect with experts in your field from around the globe **(http://connect.iste.org/home)**. There are many different networks to join (depending on your professional interests) where you can ask questions, learn from colleagues, and get access to exclusive events and professional learning opportunities. ISTE also offers free Strategic Learning Programs with partners like NASA and Verizon, which can be brought to your school or district **(http://bit.ly/1PeJ97t)**. In addition, ISTE may have affiliate organizations in your area that provide professional development at seminars and conferences **(www.iste.org/affiliates)**.

- **EdTechTeacher (http://edtechteacher.org)** is another organization that provides help to teachers and schools wishing to integrate technology to create student-centered, inquiry-based learning environments. They offer keynote presentations, hands-on workshops, online courses, and live webinars for teachers, schools, and school districts—all from your computer! What is nice about EdTechTeacher is that they understand teachers and students because the people leading the professional development have been or still are in the classroom.

- **Education World (www.educationworld.com)** is a complete online resource that offers high-quality lesson plans, classroom materials, information on how to integrate technology in the classroom, as well as articles written by education experts—a great place for you to find and share ideas with other teachers.

- **Discovery Education (www.discoveryeducation.com)** supplies a plethora of digital media that is immersive and engaging, bringing the world into the classroom to give every student a chance to experience fascinating people, places, and events. All of its content is aligned to standards that can be adjusted to support your specific curriculum and classroom instruction, regardless of what technology you have in your room. Discovery Education can help you transition to a digital-age environment and even replace all of your textbooks with digital resources, if that is your ultimate goal.

Because you are reading this book, you have already started your technology journey! And you are not alone in this nationwide endeavor. Kristi Meeuwse, an Apple Distinguished Educator, offers sage advice at her blog, **iTeach with iPads (http://iteachwithipads.net)**, as you begin your exciting learning adventure. You can also read about **"How Kristi Meeuwse Teaches with iPad"** at Apple.com **(http://tinyurl.com/qxzdsbu)**. Following is just a taste of her guidance.

> Wherever you are in your classroom journey, it's important to reflect on where you are and where you've been. It's important to celebrate your successes, no matter how small, and then be willing to move forward and try new things. Daring to imagine the possibilities and being willing to change is not just transforming to your own teaching, it will transform

your classroom in ways you never thought were possible. Today we will do exciting new things. Let's get to it.

—Kristi Meeuwse (2013, http://tinyurl.com/qf22zo7)

We will continue to give you more resources for staff development in the practical ideas chapters (8-10). To learn about staff development in grades other than 3-5, look for the three other titles in this series, as they provide information to help you differentiate for students at all levels of your class. Before we dive into lesson ideas for your specific grade and subjects, however, we will discuss how to effectively read, understand, and use the CCSS standards in the next chapters.

Chapter 5

Organization of the Standards

So your state or district has implemented CCSS, and you are asking, "Now what? How can I make this instructional shift, understand these targets, and provide quality instruction for my students?"

You can't make this transition if you don't know your way around the CCSS. So let's focus on the first task: understanding the organization of the standards. While reading this chapter, you might want to explore **"Read the Standards"** on the CCSS website **(http://tinyurl.com/p9zfnwo)** as we discuss the details.

How Are the ELA Standards Organized?

The English language arts (ELA) standards are divided into six parts (see Figure 5.1), five of which are comprehensive K–12 sections (grey boxes). Then there is one specific content area section for foundational skills in Grades K–5 (white box). (The CCSS website's introduction to the ELA standards has its own **"How to Read the Standards"** section **[http://bit.ly/1ZgEHIa]** that gives more information about organization as well as three appendices of supplemental material.)

FIGURE 5.1. The CCSS English language arts standards

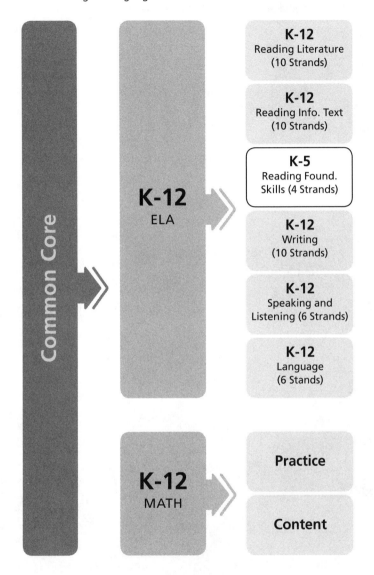

Each section is divided into strands. At the beginning of each strand is a set of College and Career Readiness (CCR) anchor standards, which are the same across all grades and content areas. Take, for example, the first anchor standard illustrated in Figure 5.2: ELA 1 (CCSS.ELA-Literacy.CCRA.R.1). It is the same in Grade 3 as it is for a fifth grader, but the grade-level standard is refined to what the student at each grade level is expected to accomplish within the anchor standard.

FIGURE 5.2. Figure 5.2. College and Career Readiness (CCR) anchor standard ELA 1 (CCSS.ELA-Literacy.CCRA.R.1) with grade-specific standards for Grades 3 and 5.

ELA Strand ➤ **ELA 1**
LITERACY KEY IDEAS AND DETAILS

College and Career Readiness Anchor Standard (CCRA) ➤ **ELA 1-CCRA**
Read closely to determine what the text says explicitly and to make logical inferences from it; cite specific textual evidence when writing or speaking to support conclusions drawn from text

ELA 1 Grade Specific Standard ➤

Grade 3 (ELA RL.3.1)
Ask and answer questions to demonstrate understanding of a text, referring explicitly to the text as the basis for the answer.

Grade 5 (ELA RL.5.1)
Quote accurately from a text when explaining what the text says explicitly and when drawing inferences from the text.

ELA 1 Anchor Standard: Read closely to determine what the text says explicitly and to make logical inferences from it; cite specific textual evidence when writing or speaking to support conclusions drawn from the text.

ELA 1 Standard in Third Grade: Ask and answer questions to demonstrate understanding of the text, referring explicitly to the text as the basis for the answers.

ELA 1 Standard in Fifth Grade: Quote accurately from the text when explaining what the text says explicitly and when drawing inferences from the text.

These anchor standards compliment the specific grade-level standards and define the skills and knowledge base that students should have by the end of each grade. The CCR standards are broad, while the grade-level standards provide specificity.

ELA standards focus on the following four areas:

1. Reading

2. Writing

3. Speaking and Listening

4. Language

The reading standards focus on text complexity (the difficulty of what students read), as well as the growth of their comprehension skills. Along with fictional stories and informational text, the CCSS focuses on poetry and dramas too. The writing standards delve into specific text types, reading response, and research. Some writing skills such as the ability to plan, revise, edit, and publish can be applied to most types of writing. Other writing skills are more specific: opinion and argumentation, informational explanatory texts, and narratives. Speaking and listening standards deal with collaboration and flexible communication. In this area, students acquire and refine their oral communication and interpersonal skills, perhaps demonstrating these skills through formal presentations.

The language standards concentrate on vocabulary, conventions, and effective use. This strand not only incorporates the essential "rules" of standard written and spoken English but also helps students to understand how language functions in different contexts. Making effective choices in meaning and style leads to better comprehension when reading and listening. The vocabulary part of this strand clarifies and/or determines the meaning of unknown and multiple-definition words and phrases by using the appropriate context clues and/or reference materials as needed. This strand also helps students demonstrate an understanding of figurative language, word relationships, and nuances in word meanings. In addition, students will be able to acquire and accurately use a range of general and domain-specific words and phrases in any academic area. (We'll talk more about domains later in this chapter, in the math standards section.)

With the organization in mind, let's learn how you, as an individual teacher, use the CCSS in ELA.

How Do You Find ELA Standards by Subject and Grade?

Since most elementary teachers teach just one grade level, the standards are organized so that you can focus on your specific area. But it is very helpful to look back at the level before you and look ahead to the standards that come next, to put your grade-level curriculum in context. (If you would like to look at a grade not included in this book, please refer to the other titles in this series.)

Using the main "English Language Arts Standards" page on the CCSS website is probably the most efficient way to find your grade- and subject-level standards **(www.corestandards.org/ELA-Literacy)**. If you know what you are looking for, the corresponding reference numbers are useful. Here is a quick introduction:

All standards that relate to literature, informational text, writing, speaking, listening, language, history/social studies, and science & technical begin with "CCSS. ELA-Literacy." The difference comes at the end, with the numbering system.

Let's use the following as an example.

CCSS.ELA-Literacy.RL.4.1

- **CCSS** is the abbreviation for Common Core State Standard.

- **ELA-Literacy** identifies this as an English language arts standard.

- **RL** stands for "reading literature."

- **4** is the grade.

- **1** is the strand.

CCSS.ELA-Literacy.SL.5.5

- **CCSS.ELA-Literacy** represents the same information as in the previous example.

- **SL** means "speaking and listening."

- The first **5** is the grade.

- The second **5** is the strand.

But there are standards within standards that are not easily apparent at first glance. For instance, there may be a reading standard that uses a historical or science text, or a speaking-and-listening standard that has a technology component to it. This book focuses on where technology is required in the CCSS, and there is plenty of technology to discuss in ELA and math!

You may be wondering how you will be able to keep all of this straight. After all, we haven't even started talking about math! We invite you to go online to view the math standards **(www.corestandards.org/Math)** as you read this next section.

How Does the Organization of Math Standards Differ?

When you look at the math standards, you will see immediately that they were written by a different group of individuals; they do not integrate other subjects like the ELA standards. Even the technology standard is separate. And the system of organization is different too. The authors of the math standards also state that the grade-level order can be changed. After the following overview, we will help you sort it all out.

For more than a decade, it has been widely reported that math curriculum in the United States is not even close to being on the same level as math education in high-performing countries. The consensus: U.S. math education needs to become substantially more focused and coherent to improve. To solve this, the CCSS were written to be clear, specific, and rigorous. Not only do the Common Core math standards stress conceptual understanding of key ideas but they continually return to the main organizing principles (place value and properties of operations) to structure those ideas. It is important to note that these new standards address what students should understand and be able to do in their study of mathematics. But asking a student to understand something also means asking a teacher to assess whether a student understands it. Therefore, we need to break apart these standards to enhance readability and to gauge what Common Core math comprehension looks like—so your students will be able to understand and you will be able to assess.

First, you need to understand that in grades K–5, the standards provide a solid foundation in whole numbers, addition, subtraction, multiplication, division, fractions, and decimals. Also, instead of covering a myriad of topics, your students will be required to immerse themselves in deep comprehension by applying mathematics to problems they have not encountered previously.

The CCSS for math begin with eight Standards for Mathematical Practice **(SMP)** **(www.corestandards.org/Math/Practice)**, which apply to all grades, K–12. These standards represent ways in which students will be engaged with math content, processes, and proficiencies—longstanding, important practices. The eight SMP are:

1. Make sense of problems and persevere in solving them.

2. Reason abstractly and quantitatively.

3. Construct viable arguments and critique the reasoning of others.

4. Model with mathematics.

5. Use appropriate tools strategically.

6. Attend to precision.

7. Look for and make use of structure.

8. Look for and express regularity in repeated reasoning.

For kindergarten through eighth grade, there are also grade-specific standards. Each contains a number of domains. Domains are larger groups of related standards that are sometimes broken into clusters. Clusters are summarized groups of related standards that fall under the main standard (see the cluster that follows the standard in Figure 5.3). Due to the connected nature of math, you may see closely related clusters in other domains as well. You can read more about this on the **"How to Read Grade-Level Standards"** page **(http://bit.ly/1sPykwd)** of the CCSS website's math standards introduction.

The grade-specific domains for Grades 3–5 are the following:

• Operations and Algebraic Thinking (K-5)

- Number and Operations in Base Ten (K-5)

- Number and Operations–Fractions (3-5)

- Measurement and Data (K-5)

- Geometry (K-8)

Here is an example of how domains are used to organize the math standards:

CCSS.Math.Content.3.NBT.A.1

- **CCSS** is the abbreviation for Common Core State Standard.

- **Math.Content** identifies that this is a math standard.

- **3.NBT** is the domain (Grade 3–Number and Operations in Base Ten).

- **A.1** is the identifier for the related standard (or cluster) under the main standard–in this case "Use place value understanding and properties of operations to perform multidigit arithmetic" (see Figure 5.3).

Now that you know how to identify a math standard and its numbering system, let's look at the following figure to see the way in which this standard is actually presented in this domain.

TABLE 5.3. Example of a standard in the third grade domain of Number and Operations in Base Ten

DOMAIN	STANDARD	CLUSTER
Grade 3 **Number and Operations in Base Ten**	Use place value understanding and properties of operations to perform multidigit arithmetic.	**CCSS.Math.Content.3.NBT.A.1:** Use place value understanding to round whole numbers to the nearest 10 or 100. **CCSS.Math.Content.3.NBT.A.2:** Fluently add and subtract within 1000 using strategies and algorithms based on place value, properties of operations, and/or the relationship between addition and subtraction. **CCSS.Math.Content.3.NBT.A.3:** Multiply one-digit whole numbers by multiples of 10 in the range 10-90 (e.g., 9 x 80, 5 x 60) using strategies based on place value and properties of operations.

The standard in Figure 5.3 defines what your students should know and be able to do after you have taught and assessed that standard. Reading and familiarizing yourself with the standards will go a long way in helping you teach the standards later.

There are also SMPs that are part of the College and Career Readiness (CCR) anchor standards of the ELA. These standards are not overtly assessed but are necessary for you to include in your instruction. SMPs will not be the focus of this book except when they involve technology.

As you can see, math and ELA standards are written and organized very differently. We have tried our best to guide you through these differences, but we do recommend that you explore the resources we have provided here as well as others that we have referenced on **our website (http://tinyurl.com/oexfhcv)**. Here are two great resources that will explain the standards of mathematical practices: **http://tinyurl.com/l3zzsae; http://tinyurl.com/9ndshh6**. In the next chapter, we discuss technology and how it relates to the CCSS.

Chapter 6

Technology Standards in the Common Core

This chapter focuses on the CCSS English language arts and math standards that have technology-related components written into them, first identifying and then analyzing these standards. This will prepare you for later chapters, where we offer practical examples of how you can integrate these standards into your curriculum.

As CCSS coaches, we know that there are those of you who are excited about technology, those of you who think it is an annoyance, and those of you who fear it. These new standards will affect all of you because they force your districts and you, as teachers, to use technology more pervasively. Schools will feel pressure to address areas that may have been avoided in the past due to cost or apprehension. If you are a fan of technology, you will welcome the changes; if you are not, you will need to become proficient. You can no longer avoid technology in your classroom.

Where Is Technology in the ELA Standards?

The CCSS are designed to prepare students for college, the workforce, and a technology-rich society. And as you learned in the last chapter, the ELA standards have the CCR (College and Career Readiness) anchor standards—reading, writing,

ELA Standards (Grades 3–5) in Which Technology Appears

READING (3–5)

- CCR Reading (R) Standard 7 **(http://tinyurl.com/h9n9ek9)**

  - Reading Literature (RL)

  - Reading Informational Text (RI)

- CCR Reading (R) Standard 5 **(http://tinyurl.com/z7cqpqj)**

Note: We will get into more detail about related anchor standard R.5 later in this chapter.

WRITING (3–5)

- CCR Writing (W) Standard 2 **(http://tinyurl.com/zt6kysv)**

- CCR Writing (W) Standard 6 **(http://tinyurl.com/zmxfdp8)**

- CCR Writing (W) Standard 8 **(http://tinyurl.com/jercjbv)**

SPEAKING AND LISTENING (3–5)

- CCR Speaking and Listening (SL) Standard 2 **(http://tinyurl.com/gvdrr3g)**

- CCR Speaking and Listening (SL) Standard 5 **(http://tinyurl.com/hrw3bdu)**

LANGUAGE (3–5)

- CCR Language (L) Standard 4 **(http://tinyurl.com/hmu54nx)**

speaking and listening, and language—at their core. Following is a summary of those CCR standards that are embedded with technology in Grades 3-5.

Where Is Technology in the Math Standards?

As mentioned in Chapter 5, the math standards are written differently, and the technology standard in math (yes, just one standard) is separate from the rest of the math standards. However, this technology standard is meant to be used ubiquitously. Though many math standards do not overtly say that technology is required, if there is a need for a calculator or statistical analysis using a computer then that is what students should use. In math, the understanding is that these technology tools are used across grade levels and throughout the math standards even though there is only one written standard about it. (Note: This math standard is presented in detail after the grade-specific ELA standards at the end of this chapter.)

What about Using Technology in All Subjects?

Because technology is integrated throughout the CCSS, we should discuss in more depth what this actually means as you go about implementing the curriculum day to day. Though the standards give you specific language, the use of technology has been left wide open. They use terms like "digital tools," "other media," and "both print and digital" to let you, as the teacher, choose what is appropriate to the lesson. The new standards are trying to infuse technology into everyday classroom use, as opposed to having a separate period in a computer lab or someplace you send the students while you have planning time are meeting, planning, or collaborating with colleagues. Technology will need to become like the pencil: just another tool to choose from when students need to find the most appropriate one to complete the task at hand.

CCSS strongly encourages project-based lessons and is built to be cross-curricular. Also, Common Core is looking for higher-level thinking, learning, and application. All of these things lead to the use of technology as the most appropriate tool in many situations. They fit very well into P21's (Partnership for 21st Century Learning's) **Framework for 21st Century Learning (http://tinyurl.com/nzvwyen)** and the **ISTE Standards for Students (www.iste.org/standards)**. So if you have been working for some time on lessons that integrate technology and you think you will have to begin again, you will be relieved to know that the new standards are not so different.

How Do You Put ELA Technology Standards into Context?

When you look at the patterns of technology use in the standards, you improve your integration planning and learning achievements with these standards. Let's take a quick look at the technology patterns in the related Grade 3–5 standards.

R.7: This is the main technology standard in reading, but the CCSS does not expect students to use technology until grade 2. The standard then continues to develop in all subsequent grades, integrating and evaluating content in various technology formats that support the meaning of a story or literary work.

RL.7: This standard begins in kindergarten, comparing illustrations and text, and then grows through the grades, using all types of media to compare, support, and analyze the story's meaning. Essentially, the purpose of the standard is to get meaning from more than the text. Meaning can also come from all the accompanying media and even the format of the story.

RI.7: This is similar to RL.7 but refers to informational text, history, and science and technical. Thus, you must keep in mind informational graphics—maps; photographs; diagrams; charts; and other media in history, technology, and science—and the way in which they augment information or help to solve a problem.

RI.5: Beginning in kindergarten with learning the parts of a book, this standard grows through third grade to an analysis of text structure. Of course, informational text in the 21st century is not only in book form. Getting meaning through the use of electronic menus and graphics in digital media is an important skill that must also be taught.

W.2: From drawing, writing, and telling about a topic in kindergarten, this standard evolves into producing a thesis in high school. It is your basic research paper that now includes an expectation to use any and all media that is appropriate to conveying the information.

W.6: This is one of the few anchor standards that is solely technology driven. From kindergarten through high school, students are required to use technology to collaborate with others when writing. Of course, this requires keyboarding skills, but they are not mentioned in the standard until Grade 3.

W.8: The use of technology in this standard is expected from Grade 3 through high school. It keys in on the gathering of information, the analysis of information, and the avoidance of plagiarism using multiple sources—digital as well as text—when writing informative or explanatory works. This standard works in tandem with standard W.2 and will probably be taught jointly.

SL.2: This standard expects the use of technology from kindergarten through Grade 12. It is a listening standard, but in today's world, all kinds of diverse media are constantly available. Students need to be able to analyze and make decisions about this content.

SL.5: Beginning with the use of pictures when speaking in kindergarten, this standard builds to making strategic use of digital media for presentations in high school. Learning to use media in presentations is critical for college and career readiness.

L.4: This is a very straightforward standard that clarifies the meaning of words at all grade levels. Starting in second grade, students need to know how to find word meanings using not just print but digital dictionaries, glossaries, and thesauruses.

What about Assessment?

You don't begin a trip without an end in mind, and the end that must always be kept in mind with the CCSS is the standardized test your state will be administering. Whether it is the PARCC or Smarter Balanced assessment, or some other assessment your state is developing, there will certainly be a technology component. This, of course, depends on your state and district. In fact, the tests that are being developed will expect students to write short passages using the computer starting in third grade. This is just one example of an assessment (keyboarding) that is not overtly stated as a standard in kindergarten, first grade, or second grade but is expected as a performance outcome in third grade. We, as educators, know you can't start teaching keyboarding in Grade 3 and expect students to be proficient in Grade 3. So it is important to start with the end in mind.

The tests will require some level of competence in selecting and highlighting text, dragging and dropping text, and moving objects on the screen. In the math areas of the test, tools that might be needed for the exam (calculators, rulers, a slide rule) will be available on the screen. Students may need headphones and a microphone to interact during the speaking-and-listening sections, and other multimedia may be used in other parts of the test.

The best way to prepare students is to know in advance the scope of technology they will need to master, but this will not be easy during the first years of rollout. Many things will be changing and many details will still be forthcoming. The tight deadline means your students may not be as fully prepared as you would like them to be. However, your preparation— giving students opportunities to use a myriad of technology as often as possible—will help them to be as ready as they can be for the assessments.

What Are the ELA Standards with Technology?

The following is a listing of where technology appears in the CCSS. The first section contains the anchor standards, and the second section has the more specific grade-level standards. The standards are in order by level so that you can find those that relate to the grade you teach more quickly. The part of the standard that pertains to technology is in boldface type. It is always helpful to look at the standards above and below your level to see where the students have come from and where they are going on their educational journey. Please refer to the other books in this series if you would like to see other grade levels.

READING
CCSS.ELA-Literacy.CCRA.R.7

R.7: Integrate and evaluate content presented in **diverse media and formats**, including visually and quantitatively, as well as in words.

Note R.5 as well: Analyze the structure of texts, including how specific sentences, paragraphs, and larger portions of the text (e.g., a section, chapter, scene, or stanza) relate to each other and the whole.

The R.5 anchor standard does not have any multimedia but does overtly include technology in its informational-text (RI) strand concerning the use of electronic texts from Grades 1–3 (**RI.1.5, RI.2.5, RI.3.5**), then has a non-technical focus in **RI.4.5** and **RI.5.5**.

WRITING
CCSS.ELA-Literacy.CCRA.W.6 and CCSS.ELA-Literacy.CCRA.W.8

W.6: Use technology, including the internet, to produce and publish writing and to interact and collaborate with others.

W.8: Gather relevant information from multiple print and **digital sources**, assess the credibility and accuracy of each source, and integrate the information while avoiding plagiarism.

Note: Anchor standard W.2 does not have multimedia but does include technology in its strand starting in Grade 4 (**W.4.2.a**).

SPEAKING AND LISTENING
CCSS.ELA-Literacy.CCRA.SL.2 and CCSS.ELA-Literacy.CCRA.SL.5

SL.2: Integrate and evaluate information presented in **diverse media and formats**, including visually, quantitatively, and orally.

SL.5: Make strategic use of **digital media and visual displays of data** to express information and enhance understanding of presentations.

Even when your grade does not have a technology standard included in these main anchor strands (**R.7, W.2, W.6, W.8, SL.2, SL.5, L.4**), it is implied that it be used. We have listed here only those that state a technology use. For instance, the first time that **RI.7** overtly states the use of technology is in Grade 4 (**RI.4.7**); but because it is in the anchor standard, it is implied that technology be used in standard **RI.7** in Grades 1–3 (**RI.1.7, RI.2.7, RI.3.7**) whenever it is appropriate to use it.

What are the ELA Grade-Level Standards with Technology?

Following is where the ELA grade-level standards appear in the CCSS (listed by grade). Note the following abbreviations: reading literature (RL), reading informational text (RI), writing (W), speaking and listening (SL), and language (L). We are including one grade below and above to give the technology standards some context. Please refer to the other books in this series to get a sense of the full scope of technology standards, Grades K–12. (Note: As in the preceding section, the part of the standard that pertains to technology is in boldface type.)

GRADE 2

RL.2.7: Use information gained from the illustrations and words in a print or **digital text** to demonstrate understanding of its characters, setting, or plot.

RI.2.5: Know and use various text features (e.g., captions, bold print, subheadings, glossaries, indexes, **electronic menus, icons**) to locate key facts or information in a text efficiently.

W.2.6: With guidance and support from adults, use a variety of **digital tools** to produce and publish writing, including in collaboration with peers.

SL.2.2: Recount or describe key ideas or details from a text read aloud or information presented orally or through **other media**.

SL.2.5: Create **audio recordings** of stories or poems; add drawings or other **visual displays** to stories or recounts of experiences when appropriate to clarify ideas, thoughts, and feelings.

L.2.4.e: Use glossaries and beginning dictionaries, **both print and digital**, to determine or clarify the meaning of words and phrases.

GRADE 3

RI.3.5: Use text features and **search tools (e.g., key words, sidebars, hyperlinks)** to locate information relevant to a given topic efficiently.

W.3.6: With guidance and support from adults, use **technology** to produce and publish writing (using **keyboarding skills**) as well as to interact and collaborate with others.

W.3.8: Recall information from experiences or gather information from print and **digital sources**; take brief notes on sources and sort evidence into provided categories.

SL.3.2: Determine the main ideas and supporting details of a text read aloud or information presented in **diverse media and formats**, including visually, quantitatively, and orally.

SL.3.5: Create engaging **audio recordings** of stories or poems that demonstrate fluid reading at an understandable pace; add **visual displays** when appropriate to emphasize or enhance certain facts or details.

L.3.4.d: Use glossaries or beginning dictionaries, both print and **digital**, to determine or clarify the precise meaning of key words and phrases.

GRADE 4

RL.4.7: Make connections between the text of a story or drama and a **visual** or oral **presentation** of the text, identifying where each version reflects specific descriptions and directions in the text.

RI.4.7: Interpret information presented visually, orally, or quantitatively (e.g., in charts, graphs, diagrams, time lines, **animations**, or **interactive elements on webpages**) and explain how the information contributes to an understanding of the text in which it appears.

W.4.2.a: Introduce a topic clearly and group related information in paragraphs and sections; include formatting (e.g., headings), illustrations, and **multimedia** when useful to aiding comprehension.

W.4.6: With some guidance and support from adults, use **technology, including the internet**, to produce and publish writing as well as to interact and collaborate with others; demonstrate sufficient command of **keyboarding skills** to type a minimum of one page in a single sitting.

W.4.8: Recall relevant information from experiences or gather relevant information from print and **digital sources**; take notes and categorize information, and provide a list of sources.

SL.4.2: Paraphrase portions of a text read aloud or information presented in **diverse media and formats**, including visually, quantitatively, and orally.

SL.4.5: Add **audio recordings and visual displays** to presentations when appropriate to enhance the development of main ideas or themes.

L.4.4.c: Consult reference materials (e.g., dictionaries, glossaries, thesauruses), both print and **digital**, to find the pronunciation and determine or clarify the precise meaning of key words and phrases.

GRADE 5

RL.5.7: Analyze how visual and **multimedia elements** contribute to the meaning, tone, or beauty of a text (e.g., graphic novel, **multimedia presentation** of fiction, folktale, myth, poem).

RI.5.7: Draw on information from multiple print or **digital sources**, demonstrating the ability to locate an answer to a question quickly or to solve a problem efficiently.

W.5.2.a: Introduce a topic clearly, provide a general observation and focus, and group related information logically; include formatting (e.g., headings), illustrations, and **multimedia** when useful to aiding comprehension.

W.5.6: With some guidance and support from adults, use **technology, including the Internet**, to produce and publish writing as well as to interact and collaborate with others; demonstrate sufficient command of **keyboarding skills** to type a minimum of two pages in a single sitting.

W.5.8: Recall relevant information from experiences or gather relevant information from print and **digital sources**; summarize or paraphrase information in notes and finished work, and provide a list of sources.

SL.5.2: Summarize a written text read aloud or information presented in **diverse media and formats**, including visually, quantitatively, and orally.

SL.5.5: Include **multimedia components (e.g., graphics, sound) and visual displays** in presentations when appropriate to enhance the development of main ideas or themes.

L.5.4.c: Consult reference materials (e.g., dictionaries, glossaries, thesauruses), both print and **digital**, to find the pronunciation and determine or clarify the precise meaning of key words and phrases.

GRADE 6

RL.6.7: Compare and contrast the experience of reading a story, drama, or poem to **listening to or viewing an audio, video,** or live version of the text, including contrasting what they "see" and "hear" when reading the text to what they perceive when they listen or watch.

RI.6.7: Integrate information presented in **different media or formats** (e.g., visually, quantitatively) as well as in words to develop a coherent understanding of a topic or issue.

W.6.2.a: Introduce a topic; organize ideas, concepts, and information using strategies such as definition, classification, comparison/contrast, and cause/effect; include formatting (e.g., headings), graphics (e.g., charts, tables), and **multimedia** when useful to aiding comprehension.

W.6.6: Use **technology, including the internet**, to produce and publish writing as well as to interact and collaborate with others; demonstrate sufficient command of **keyboarding skills** to type a minimum of three pages in a single sitting.

W.6.8: Gather relevant information from multiple print and **digital sources**; assess the credibility of each source; and quote or paraphrase the data and conclusions of others while avoiding plagiarism and providing basic bibliographic information for sources.

SL.6.2: Interpret information presented in **diverse media and formats** (e.g., visually, quantitatively, orally) and explain how it contributes to a topic, text, or issue under study.

SL.6.5: Include **multimedia components (e.g., graphics, images, music, sound) and visual displays** in presentations to clarify information.

L.6.4.c: Consult reference materials (e.g., dictionaries, glossaries, thesauruses), both print and **digital**, to find the pronunciation of a word or determine or clarify its precise meaning or its part of speech.

What Is the Math Standard with Technology?

The Standards for Mathematical Practice (SMP) are skills that all of your students should look to develop. As you learned in Chapter 5, there are eight SMP, which are designed to overlay the math content standards. In other words, math practice standards apply to every one of the math content standards. So, although **MP5** is the only standard that includes technology, it actually means that every math content standard should use the appropriate tools, including tools that use technology.

Following is **MP5**, taken verbatim from the Common Core State Standards website. As in the preceding two sections, any text that pertains to technology is in boldface type.

CCSS.MATH.PRACTICE.MP5

MP5: Use **appropriate tools** strategically.

Mathematically proficient students consider the available tools when solving a mathematical problem. These tools might include pencil and paper, concrete models, a ruler, a protractor, **a calculator, a spreadsheet, a computer algebra system, a statistical package, or dynamic geometry software**. Proficient students are sufficiently familiar with tools appropriate for their grade or course to make sound decisions about when each of these tools might be helpful, recognizing both the insight to be gained and their limitations. For example, mathematically proficient high school students analyze graphs of functions and solutions generated using a **graphing calculator**. They detect possible errors by strategically using estimation and other mathematical knowledge. When making mathematical models, they know that **technology** can enable them to visualize the results of varying assumptions, explore consequences, and compare predictions with data. Mathematically proficient students at various grade levels are able to identify relevant external mathematical resources, such as **digital content located on a website**, and use them to pose or solve problems. They are able to use **technological tools** to explore and deepen their understanding of concepts.

It is important to note the standard's emphasis on using technology pervasively. Keep technology in mind, not only when teaching the standards but in the assessment, as it creates a learning advantage for your students.

We hope you have taken away important information on where technology can be found in the CCSS. In the next chapter, we discuss practical strategies and offer helpful resources so you can begin teaching the CCSS right away.

Chapter 7

Implementing Practical Ideas

Our world and education is changing rapidly. Without question, one size does not fit all in teaching. We know you work hard to personalize the learning in your classroom to reflect the individual needs, capabilities, and learning styles of your students so they have opportunities to reach their maximum potential. With this in mind, why not create tech-savvy classrooms for today's students?

In this chapter, we address practical ways to use new technology ideas within your classroom. Most of your students already come to school with a strong background in and understanding of technology. They are interested, motivated, and even driven by technology. Having a tech-savvy classroom for today's students is the best way to create a digital-age learning environment.

How and Where do I Begin?

Whether you are a new teacher, a teacher in the middle of a career, or a veteran teacher with just a few years before retirement, you will begin at the same place in respect to technology. To bring technology into your classrooms and your students into the digital age, you must give up your role at the front of class and let technology be a primary source of information. This journey calls for no longer teaching in the way you've been teaching and instead becoming a facilitator of your classroom and the information presented there. Embrace all of the devices you have ignored or struggled to keep out of your classroom. Introduce yourself to new concepts that may not have existed when you were in school.

First, sign up for as many technology teaching blogs and websites as you can find. One website definitely worth a look is **Power My Learning (www.powermylearning. org)**. There are many free activities for you to explore, and you can search for lessons by the CCSS. This website also allows you to build classes, assign and monitor student work, and customize playlists for your classroom.

Blogs are becoming an increasingly pervasive and persistent influence in people's lives. They are a great way to allow individual participation in the marketplace of ideas around the world. Teachers have picked up on the creative use of this technology and put the blog to work in the classroom. The education blog can be a powerful and effective tool for students and teachers. **Edutopia** has a wonderful technology blog **(http://tinyurl.com/p33sd7b)**. **Scholastic** also offers a blog for teachers, PK–12, **(http://tinyurl.com/oaaycar)** and on a wide variety of educational topics.

Edmodo (www.edmodo.com) is a free and easy blog for students and teachers to communicate back and forth. We have given you links to all of these resources on **our website (http://tinyurl.com/oexfhcv)**, which serves as a companion for this book. Teachers can post assignments and students can respond to the teacher, as well as to each other, either in the classroom or at home. Students have the ability to also post questions to the teacher or one another, if they need help.

What Strategies Can I Use?

Get a routine going. Centers, where students are engaged in independent and self-directed learning activities, are a great way to begin integrating technology in your classroom. All centers can be tied to your curriculum targets and a couple of them can be technology based. There ar e a plethora of computer based games that you can bring to a center rotation. **ScootPad (www.scootpad.com)** and **DreamBox (www. dreambox.com)** are two programs that support Common Core and can be used on computers or tablets.

Differentiated math instruction meets the needs of all learners. It consists of, whole group, mini lessons, guided math groups, and independent learning stations with a wide variety of activities, and ongoing assessment. Independent learning stations are a great way to infuse technology into your centers. One station with computers and another with games make great rotation centers and are easy to plan for, as well as a great way for students to practice math fluency and target related games. For more information on how to set up a guided math classroom check out the book *Guided Math: A Framework for Mathematics Instruction* (2009) by Laney Sammons or view her **guided math slide presentation** online **(www.slideshare.net/ggierhart/ guided-math-powerpointbytheauthorofguidedmath)**.

Guided Reading is a key component of Balanced Literacy instruction. The teacher meets with a small group of students, reading and instructing them at their level. Other students are involved in small groups or independent practice that involves reading, writing, or vocabulary. **Reading A-Z (www.readinga-z)** offers many literacy-based books and games that can be used in reading centers. Students can use recording devices to record and listen to themselves reading. You can also listen to their recordings for quick assessment purposes. Reading A-Z also offers **Vocabulary A-Z** and **Science A-Z**. There are many games and activities for these content areas, and this offers you additional rotations for your literacy centers.

Programs and apps, such as Google docs, Puppet Pals, and Comic Life, are just a few resources you can use to meet standards and bring writing into your literacy rotations. Your students are using technology to be creative.

Flipping the classroom is another great way to integrate technology into your classroom. This teaching model, which uses both online and face-to-face instruction, is transforming education. Flipping is an educational strategy that provides students with the chance to access information within a subject outside of the classroom. Instead of students listening in class to content and then practicing that concept outside of the school day, that traditional practice is flipped. Students work with information whenever it best fits their schedule, and as many times as necessary for learning to occur. Inside the flipped classroom, teachers and students engage in discussion, practice, or experiential learning. By creating online tutorials of your instruction, using some of the tools mentioned in this book, you can spend valuable class time assisting students with homework, conferencing about learning, or simply being available for student questions.

Pick an app or program you are interested in bringing into your classroom. Play and explore. See what the possibilities are for using this technology in your classroom. You and your students can be technology pioneers. Allow your students to problem solve and seek new knowledge on their own and then have them share with you. A great resource to use is **iPad in Education (www.apple.com/education/ipad)**, where you can learn more about how to teach with and use iPads in your classroom. This site from Apple is a great resource—it gives you lots of information about what the iPad is capable of, gives examples of iPad lessons done by other teachers, and offers free apps!

How Do I Determine What Works Best?

Perhaps the next place to look is the **ISTE Standards for Students**, which were developed by the International Society for Technology in Education (ISTE) and can be found on their website **(iste.org/standards)**. These standards are a great framework to help you plan lessons and projects to support the Common Core technology standards in literacy, math, and critical thinking skills.

The Partnership for 21st Century Skills developed a Framework for 21st Century Learning. This framework identifies key skills known as the 4Cs: Critical Thinking, Collaboration, Communication, and Creativity. Table 7.1 takes those four skills and overlays them with digital resources that you can use in English language arts (ELA). For instance, if you are a third grade teacher and want to use Collaboration in your lesson, you might try any of the seven digital resources suggested to plan the lesson: Google Docs, Popplet, GarageBand, Wixie, Edmodo, wikis, and Google Sites. These are suggestions, but there are many more apps and sites that might also fit well. You might notice that the 4Cs mirror many of the ISTE standards. This table is included to get you to think about how you can include the 4Cs and technology in your daily lesson planning.

Being an expert on all of the apps or programs listed in Table 7.1 is not necessary. Start with one you know, or find out which ones your students are familiar with and start there. Think about the target or lesson you want to teach. What is the goal? What technology device or app or program will support your teaching? Create an

TABLE 7.1. How Digital Resources for ELA Fit into the 4C's.

GRADE	CRITICAL THINKING	COLLABORATION	COMMUNICATION	CREATIVITY
3-5	**BrainPOP** **DreamBox Learning** **ScootPad** **Reading/Science/ A-Z**	**Google Docs** **Popplet** **GarageBand** **Wixie** **Edmodo** **Wikis** **Google Sites**	**Edmodo** **Skype** **Explain Everything** **Show Me** **Puppet Pals** **GarageBand** **Wixie**	**Comic Life** **Puppet Pals** **Wixie** **GarageBand** **iMovie** **Keynote**

end product to show your students what you expect. Instead of step-by-step teaching of the technology, it is important to let the students explore and discover for themselves, as long as your end product and expectations have been met.

You can also teach yourself about many of the apps or programs available by searching for them online. YouTube also has step-by-step how-to videos for many tech apps and programs. Have your students show what they know by creating samples for you. Save everything you, your colleagues, or your students create, and keep it all in a digital portfolio, so you can share the samples with your students for years to come.

With an active learning environment and providing the tools your students need for 21st-century learning, watch the difference you will make as learning in your classroom skyrockets. All of this new technology is transforming today's classrooms. Social networking and mobile learning are just a few tech-related activities that students and teachers are embracing. The website for this book **(http://tinyurl.com/ oexfhcv)** contains further lists of resources for how to incorporate the technology you have (or want to have) and ways for your students to learn and interact with it. In the following chapters, we further explore the standards for 3–5 that incorporate technology, suggest specific applications and strategies, and provide lessons to help students successfully achieve those standards.

Chapter 8

Practical Ideas for Third Grade

We realize that you will want to focus on your particular grade or subject when you are planning your lessons and implementing CCSS, so we have organized the practical ideas chapters by grade level, then subject. Each grade starts with an overview followed by ELA technology standards with accompanying apps, software, and websites that you can use to help your students succeed with that standard. We then continue with the math standard for the grade level, also with accompanying resources. Finally, we have included some sample lessons for each grade level in various subject areas. Although we intend for you to seek your specific grade and subject to help you implement CCSS for your students, please do not disregard other sections of this chapter. To see grades other than 3–5, look for our three additional titles in this collection, as they could provide information to help you differentiate for students at all levels of your class.

The CCSS expect third graders to use technology to enhance their literacy skills. The literacy standards place an emphasis on information gathering and publishing of student writing. Students should also use technology to practice math skills. This includes the use of digital math tools in the form of software programs, apps, or websites. We have pulled out the third grade standards that include technology and list them in this chapter. We also offer ideas and suggestions for which technologies to use and how to teach with them.

Research Ideas

> **RI.3.5** | READING INFORMATION
>
> Use text features and **search tools** (e.g., **keywords, sidebars, hyperlinks**) to locate information relevant to a given topic efficiently

> **W.3.8** | WRITING
>
> Recall information from experiences or gather information from print and **digital sources**; take brief notes on sources and sort evidence into provided categories.

WE HAVE COMBINED RI.3.5 WITH W.3.8 because search tools will also be used when gathering information from digital sources. In third grade, students need to use search tools to find relevant information on the internet. They will need to be taught the features of webpages and how to navigate through them. Understanding the layout of webpages, such as the functions of sidebars and hyperlinks, is also necessary. The best way to do this is to show various webpages (using websites from your literacy or science standards will be a great way to integrate your curriculum with this technology standard), then model and explain what the features are and their functions by using an interactive whiteboard. Don't have an interactive whiteboard? Check out a free site called **RealtimeBoard (www.realtime-board.com)**. All you need is a computer and a projector to run this virtual online whiteboard.

Teaching students which keywords to use and how to analyze search results will definitely help them find better sources and think more critically about any information they find on the internet. Following are some tips to help when teaching students to conduct a search.

- Choose your search terms carefully. Be precise about what you are looking for, though you should use phrases and not full sentences.

- Adding more words can narrow a search. Use Boolean searches to narrow your topic with quotation marks. There's a big difference between the search term "gopher" and "Habitats of gophers in North America."

- Use synonyms! If students can't find what they're looking for, have them try keywords that mean the same thing or are related.

- Type "site:" Typing the word site: (with the colon) after your keyword and before a URL will tell Google to search within a specific website.

- Add a minus sign. Adding a minus sign immediately before any word, with no space in between, indicates that you don't want that word to appear in your search results. For example, "Saturn -cars" will give you information about the planet, not the automobile.

Kid-Friendly Search Engines

Protecting students from unsafe content is the most important reason for using search engines made specifically for kids. Allowing your students to have the run of the web using a search engine for young students helps you, because it is difficult to monitor an entire class that is using unfiltered search engines.

Of course, there is no guarantee that results will be safe even when using a search engine tailored for children. Many districts have filters on their networks, but if yours does not, we suggest you explore the following.

SEARCH ENGINES

- **Kids Click (www.kidsclick.org):** A web search site designed for kids by librarians with kid-friendly results. This site is free and for Grades 2–5.

- **Google for Kids (www.safesearchkids.com):** Google for Kids Safe Search Kids is a custom search engine using Google's Safe Search features with additional filtering to block more potentially harmful material than if you simply use Google. It is fun, colorful, and easy for kids to use.

- **Google Kid Search (www.kidzsearch.com):** This is another safe search engine powered by Google for Grades K–8. However, please be aware there are ads on this site.

- **Yahoo for Kids (http://tinyurl.com/nqn4p39):** Yahooligans is a safe search engine for young students (K–2) picked by editors at Yahoo.

- **Ask Kids (www.ask.com):** This is a free, filtered search engine for Grades K–6.

Using programs such as **PebbleGo (www.pebblego.com)** (must be purchased) is a great online source for PK–3 students to find easy-to-read informational text that includes citation support, videos, and audio recordings, as well as games and activities on many science topics that are typically used at this level. Although you also need to pay for it, **Power Knowledge (www.pkearthandspace.com and www.**

pklifescience.com) is another program that can be used with your third grade science topics to find easy-reading science resources.

Tried and true methods for note taking and categorizing information found in books can still be used to gather and record information on websites. Teaching students to use data sheets, note cards, and KWL (Know, What, Learn) techniques still works; however, there are now ways that technology can make this easier. The **Kentucky Virtual Library (http://tinyurl.com/ptnwz4)** is a great website to use as a resource for some of these techniques.

Mind-mapping tools will help your students organize their research when gathering information. Several wonderful software programs have been used for mind-mapping for many years. However, there are also free sites out there. Following are some digital tools you can use to teach note taking and categorizing.

NOTE-TAKING TOOLS

- **Kidspiration (http://tinyurl.com/dg2cxa):** A mind-mapping software program that helps students organize their writing. It can be especially helpful for students who are learning to create paragraphs and organize big ideas into their smaller parts. $40 to $640. Their web-based version is called Webspiration (http://tinyurl.com/bmop3nh) and costs $6/month.

- **Bubbl.us (www.bubbl.us):** This is a free (with limited use) mind-mapping website for Grades K–12. It can be shared by multiple students at a time and comes with an app. For more options, purchase a package for $6/month or $59/year. Both come with a 30-day free trial. Site licensing is available. Contact the company for specifics.

- **Mindmeister (www.mindmeister.com/education):** This is a free, basic, mind-mapping website for Grades 2–12. Upgrades are available ($18/month for a single user; $30 per user for 6 months). Educational pricing is available for schools and universities ($6 per user for 6 months). All of the upgrades have a free trial period.

- **FreeMind (http://tinyurl.com/5qrd5):** This is a free mind-mapping tool for Grades 2–12. However, FreeMind is written in Java and will run on almost any system with a Java runtime environment. Options for a basic or maximum install are available.

- **Evernote (www.evernote.com):** This is a free app that allows you to import a worksheet, document, or picture, including a snapshot of a webpage, and then annotate it using tools that you would use with interactive whiteboard software. It lets you highlight words, cut and paste, and add sticky notes. It also allows you to use voice recognition. You can then send your annotated sheet to someone else.

Of course, students can also use word processing tools, such as **Microsoft Office (www.office.com), Pages (www.apple.com/mac/pages)**, or **Google Docs (www.google.com/docs/about).** Some teachers also make digital templates to help students find specific information and to help students organize their notes.

Third graders will also need to provide a list of sources. You could make a template for sources and have students fill it in using a word processing program; however, there are websites students can use, such as **Easybib (www.easybib.com)**. Easybib is a free website and app for ages 5-12. You can use this site to generate citations in MLA, APA, and Chicago formats easily. Just copy and paste or scan the book's barcode. Students can also cite a list of sources on their own by including URL, publisher or author, topic/title, and date a website was published. If the date published is not available, they should note the date retrieved from the internet.

Writing Resources

W.3.6	WRITING
With guidance and support from adults, **use technology** to produce and publish writing (using **keyboarding skills**) as well as to interact and collaborate with others.	

MICROSOFT POWERPOINT (OFFICE.COM) IS OFTEN the presentation tool of choice—even with young students—when using technology to produce and publish writing in a collaborative way. While this is still a great program, other presentation tools have emerged. Apple offers **Keynote (www.apple.com/mac/keynote)** as part of its software package. Its features are similar to PowerPoint. Another program that has emerged is **Google Slides (www.google.com/slides/about)**. It is aimed toward business presentations; however, it is free and web-based. Google Slides make it easy to share a project that multiple users can work on at once, which makes this an especially great program to use when interacting and collaborating remotely. You can also add audio recordings to your slides, as well as visual displays such as pictures and short video clips. These can be used to enhance the development of the main ideas or theme of your presentations. Some apps can be used when beginning to produce writing.

PRESENTATION APPS

- **Toontastic (www.launchpadtoys.com):** Students use visuals to tell stories that they can collaborate on and share with others. The app Toontastic Jr. is free with a few backgrounds. Upgrade for $9.99 or purchase a classroom set, discounted depending on the number of students.

- **iMovie (www.apple.com/ios/imovie/):** This app ($4.99), which also comes as a program, has many uses in the classroom to create full edited videos or short 1-minute trailers. The trailers can be very useful for recounting and presenting ideas to others.

- **Animoto (www.animoto.com):** This website allows you to turn your photos and music into stunning video slideshows. Educational use is free for unlimited videos of 20 minutes.

- **Explain Everything (www.explaineverything.com):** This $2.99 app uses text, video, pictures, and voice to present whatever your students are asked to create. They can illustrate a story or poem or recount information they hear.

- **StoryBuddy 2 (www.tapfuze.com/storybuddy2/):** This app is easier to use than Explain Everything, but not as versatile. You can use it to create stories with pictures that can be recorded, printed, and read aloud. The price is $3.99.

- **Puppet Pals (http://tinyurl.com/qbgaks2):** This app allows students to create a puppet production using familiar characters to tell or retell a story. It is free, but for $2.99, you can get all the add-ons.

- **Sock Puppets (http://tinyurl.com/luznt6n):** This free app allows you to create a play with sock puppets, recording your student's voice and automatically syncing it to the puppet. $1.99 gets all the extras.

- **Scene Speak (http://tinyurl.com/qg55sej):** Use it to create visual scene displays and "interactive" social stories. It allows images to be edited and scenes to be linked to create "books" by theme or area of interest. The app is $9.99.

Presenting digitally is not limited to sharing with small or whole groups in the classroom. Many websites out there allow you to publish student writing to the world. Using blogging websites, such as **Edmodo (www.edmodo.com)** and **Wikispaces (www.wikispaces.com)**, is a way to share student writing in a safe, protected environment. Both Edmodo and Wikispaces allow teachers to set themselves up as administrators and add students to different groups. All of the students' writing is kept secure in these groups. You can give them assignments asking for short answers that everyone can respond to, or you can ask students to write longer pieces on their own and then submit privately to you or post writing on the site to share.

There are good software programs and sites that let you create books in print and ebook formats. There are also sites that ask students to submit their work for possible publication. The following resources are just a few of our favorites.

PUBLICATION APPS

- **PBS Kids Writing (pbskids.org/writerscontest/):** This site asks for student writing and serves as a nice incentive to get students to do their best writing. Free.

- **Lulu (www.lulu.com) and Lulu Jr (www.lulujr.com):** These sites allow you to create real books and publish them online. Parents can purchase the books as a keepsake. The site is free to use, but there is a fee to publish.

- **TikaTok (www.tikatok.com):** This is another site that allows students to write, create, and publish stories as ebooks or hardcover books. TikaTok Story Spark is an app that you can purchase for $3. Classroom price for TikaTok starts at $19 a year.

- **Poetry Idea Engine from Scholastic (http://tinyurl.com/2cuowf):** Allows you to use templates to make different forms of poetry, another great way technology gets kids writing. Better still, it is free!

Just when you should teach keyboarding is a decades-old debate. Some teachers want students to begin formalized keyboarding as young as kindergarten. Others don't believe students' hands are developmentally ready until third grade. By fourth grade, students are expected to type a page in one sitting. Therefore, whether you think children's hands are ready or not, formalized keyboarding will have to begin in the primary grades. There are many keyboarding programs you can buy. Following are some tried and true programs that we have used.

- **Mavis Beacon Keyboarding Kidz (http://tinyurl.com/254v9on):** Set words-per-minute goals; see what keys you need to practice and what keys you know well. Play games to practice what you've learned and to improve your speed and accuracy to become a typing pro. ($19.99)

- **Type to Learn (www.ttl4.sunburst.com):** This typing program, for Grades K–12, emphasizes both accuracy and words per minute speed, and provides each student with individualized remediation and goals for success. Consult the website for various pricing options and to request a quote.

- **Typing Training (www.typingtraining.com):** This web-based program with apps (for Grades 3–12) allows access from any computer or handheld device. Animated coaches are available with a customizable curriculum. Students can play games or choose from more than 2,500 unique exercises while tracking progress with detailed reports and graphs. Consult the website for various options and to request a quote.

Paying for a good typing program is worth the expense. A quality program keeps track of student progress and their levels of accomplishment. If you can't buy a program, there are many free sites that offer some instruction and games.

- **Dance Mat Typing (bbc.co.uk/guides/z3c6tfr):** This free website by BBC schools teaches typing for younger students.

- **TypingWeb (www.typing.com):** This site has ads, but it does keep track of student progress with typing skills and allows reports. Free.

- **TypeRacer (play.typeracer.com):** Free website where you can race opponents by typing words in paragraph form. For experienced typists to bone up on accuracy and typing speed. There are ads.

Some districts have students go to computer labs to practice keyboarding at given times, others fit it in where they can in the classroom, and still others have students practice and learn at home. We have found that the best way is to combine all three. Students benefit from formal keyboarding instruction, but they need to practice both in the classroom and at home. When students are working at the computers in your classroom, they need repeated reminders to keep up good techniques such as sitting up straight, keeping hands in home row, wrists slightly curved, and moving the fingers instead of the hands.

Speaking and Listening

SL.3.2	SPEAKING AND LISTENING

Determine the main ideas and supporting details of a text read aloud or information presented in **diverse media and formats**, including visually, quantitatively, and orally.

SL.3.5	SPEAKING AND LISTENING

Create engaging audio recordings of stories or poems that demonstrate fluid reading at an understandable pace; add **visual displays** when appropriate to emphasize or enhance certain facts or details.

THE TEACHER, STUDENTS, OR EVEN SOME programs can read text aloud. Sites such as **Follett Shelf (http://tinyurl.com/)** and **TumbleBooks (www.tumblebooks.com)** (must be purchased) allow you to have access to multiple ebooks, which include fiction as well as non-fiction. You can also check out many ebooks at your local library or purchase them from booksellers, such as Amazon or Barnes & Noble (especially if you have e-readers). There are also some free ebooks available. **Project Gutenberg (http://gutenberg.org/)**, **FreeReadFeed (www.freereadfeed.com)**, or **FreeBookSifter (www.freebooksifter.com)** is a possibility. There are adult titles on these sites, too, so choose carefully. Though, of course, the sites that you pay for give you a much better selection.

Using ebooks or a website with your interactive whiteboard (or free whiteboard sites) allows interaction when modeling or for student engagement. Informational text works especially well with standard **SL.3.2**; however, fictional pieces can also be used. Working with the teacher or on their own, students need to understand the main idea of text and to state supporting details. Using ebooks with your interactive whiteboard tools (highlighting main ideas and supporting details or cutting and pasting) will allow you to work with the class as a whole or a small group to help them understand the main idea. Students can then work alone or with a partner on a tablet or laptop to do the same thing that you have modeled.

Software programs can also be used to help extend thinking and learning with mind-mapping programs.

APPS TO SUPPORT MAIN IDEA

- **Kidspiration (http://tinyurl.com/dg2cxa):** A mind-mapping software program that helps students organize their writing. It can be especially helpful for students who are learning to create paragraphs and organize big ideas into their smaller parts. $40 to $640. Their web-based version is called **Webspiration (http://tinyurl.com/bmop3nh)**. $6/month.

- **Popplet (www.popplet.com):** A wonderful online organizational tool for students' writing. A free app called Popplet Lite is also available. It is easy to use, and students can import pictures and text to create web maps.

- **Bubbl.us (www.bubbl.us):** This is a free (with limited use) mind-mapping website for Grades K–12. It can be shared by multiple students at a time and comes with an accompanying app. For more options, purchase a package for $6/month or $59/year. Both come with a 30-day free trial. Site licensing is available. Contact the company for specifics.

- **Mindmeister (www.mindmeister.com/education):** This is a free, basic mind-mapping website for Grades 2–12. Upgrades are available ($18/month for a single user; $30 per user for 6 months). Educational pricing is available for schools and universities ($6 per user for 6 months). All of the upgrades have a free trial period.

- **FreeMind (http://tinyurl.com/5qrd5):** This is a free mind-mapping tool for Grades 2–12. However, FreeMind is written in Java and will run on almost any system with a Java runtime environment. Options for a basic or maximum install are available.

- **iFunFace (www.ifunface.com):** Students can create a read aloud to show how the main idea and details flow by using a photo and audio recording to create an animation. It helps students visualize how to support details that branch off from the main ideas and how they all flow together. App is free but can be upgraded for $1.99.

- **Puppet Pals (http://tinyurl.com/qbgaks2):** This app allows students to create a puppet production using familiar characters to tell or retell a story. It is free, but for $2.99 you can get all the add-ons.

Creating audio recordings and ebooks is a powerful and engaging way to demonstrate and perform fluid and accurate readings and satisfy **SL3.5**. Students can create their own audio recordings of stories or poems. You can use these recordings to check for fluency all year long.

Scanning finished book pages into **Microsoft PowerPoint (www.office.com)**, **Keynote (www.apple.com/mac/keynote)**, or **Google Slides (www.google.com/slides/about)** programs allow you to make ebooks for your classroom. Keynote allows you to speak directly into the program, and then easily stores ebooks for all students. Options include controlling the speed of page advancement, recording narration, adding action buttons, adjusting mouse-over and mouse-click actions, incorporating preset animation, and setting page transition effects.

SITES TO SUPPORT FLUENCY

- **Cast UDL Bookbuilder (http://bookbuilder.cast.org):** This is a free site, which allows students to create and share their own eBooks online. You can also read what other students have written.

- **Prezi (www.prezi.com):** You can sign up for a free educational account, and your students can create and share presentations online. Prezi has mind-mapping, zoom, and motion and can import files. Presentations can be downloaded. A Prezi viewer app is available.

- **Evernote (www.evernote.com):** This is a free app that allows you to import a worksheet, document, or picture, including a snapshot of a webpage, and then annotate it using tools that you would use with interactive whiteboard software. It lets you highlight words, cut and paste, and add sticky notes. It also allows you to use voice recognition. You can then send your annotated sheet to someone else.

- **WebQuests (www.webquest.org):** These are good tools to use for presentations. WebQuest is a website that allows students to follow an already-created, project-based lesson where information is found solely on the internet. You can also create their own WebQuest if you have a website-building program or a website like **Kafafa (www.kafafa.com/kafafa)**. WebQuest.org is the original and most popular site; however, if you search the internet, you will find more sites that you can use.

Language Resources

> **L.3.4d** | LANGUAGE
>
> Use glossaries or beginning dictionaries, both print and **digital**, to determine or clarify the precise meaning of key words and phrases.

MERRIAM-WEBSTER (MERRIAM-WEBSTER.COM), still the most commonly used dictionary, has a free and kid-friendly digital dictionary called **Kids. Wordsmyth (https://kids.wordsmyth.net/we)**. **Wordsmyth (www.wordsmyth.net)** is another good third grade option. **Little Explorers (http://tinyurl.com/2swjc)** from Enchanted Learning is a limited picture dictionary that comes with a subscription. This is a good tool to use with students who struggle with vocabulary. While digital dictionaries are not updated as often as encyclopedias, they are convenient. These sites should be bookmarked or put on your website for easy access. The more students use them, the more comfortable they will become. You should plan lessons and activities to help students learn and practice the skills needed to use an online dictionary, just as you would when using hard-copy dictionaries and glossaries.

A lesson plan idea when using electronic dictionaries is to look up difficult vocabulary words in a piece of informational text. You could give students a website (preferably on a standards topic from literacy or science) and ask them to write down all of the words they don't know. They can use an electronic dictionary to find the definitions to these words. They then reread the passage, and, with success, will come away with a better understanding of its content.

Using the app or website **Trading Cards (http://tinyurl.com/8lqftek)** is a great way to document vocabulary words by adding definitions, a picture, and recordings of pronunciations. You can also use Trading Cards as part of a fun activity that uses an online thesaurus. Simply give students a word on a trading card and then ask them to make as many trading cards as they can of synonyms and antonyms of that word. They can print these out and trade them with others or make them into a digital book.

Math Resources

THERE ARE TWO MAIN SETS OF STANDARDS—processes and practices—in the Common Core Math standards. First, you have the math targets, written similarly to ELA (Operations & Algebraic Thinking; Number & Operation in Base Ten; Numbers & Operations—Fractions; Measurement & Data; and Geometry). While you work with third grade students on mathematical processes, Operations & Algebraic Thinking, you need to teach your students how to apply the Standards for Mathematical Practices (which include problem solving and precision), to those processes. One practice, the only one that includes technology, is mathematical practice 5, "Use appropriate tools strategically."

MP5	MATH
Use appropriate **tools** strategically.	

Below is the explanation CCSS provides for **MP5**. As this is the standard explanation for Grades K–12, it does include references to higher grades.

> Mathematically proficient students consider the available tools when solving a mathematical problem. These tools might include pencil and paper, concrete models, a ruler, a protractor, **a calculator, a spreadsheet, a computer algebra system, a statistical package, or dynamic geometry software**. Proficient students are sufficiently familiar with tools appropriate for their grade or course to make sound decisions about when each of these tools might be helpful, recognizing both the insight to be gained and their limitations. For example, mathematically proficient high school students analyze graphs of functions and solutions generated using a **graphing calculator**. They detect possible errors by strategically using estimation and other mathematical knowledge. When making mathematical models, they know that technology can enable them to visualize the results of varying assumptions, explore consequences, and compare predictions with data. Mathematically proficient students at various grade levels are able to identify relevant external mathematical resources, such as **digital content located on a website**, and use them to pose or solve problems. They are able to use **technological tools** to explore and deepen their understanding of concepts.

Because this description did not give examples for all grades, we have provided a list of appropriate apps, websites, software, and lessons that will help translate this standard for third grade.

Your students will be using technology as a tool to help them become better at math. That is essentially what this math standard, the only one that explicitly includes technology, states. Many math programs, websites, and apps allow students to explore and deepen their understanding of math concepts. The best of them have students learning in creative ways and are not just electronic worksheets. They automatically adapt to the students' skill levels, and they give you the data you need to know where they are in their learning and what students need to effectively continue. Of course, these usually do not come free. Following are many good math resources. Some are free; some are not. The free resources, many with ads, are unfortunately usually less interesting to your students and not as well organized. They don't give you the feedback you need. It is up to you to decide what is best for your circumstances and budget.

Following are some resources we recommend for teaching to the third grade math standards.

WEBSITES FOR MATH

- **ScootPad (www.scootpad.com):** This is a web-based math site that is customizable for individual students. It adapts to the student and keeps the teacher in the loop with multiple reports. It is completely aligned to the CCSS. The price for a class varies from $5 to $20/month.

- **DreamBox Learning Math (www.dreambox.com):** Individualized, adaptive game-based math resource that keeps kids coming back for more. Available online or through an app. Price is $12.95/month (home) or $25/month (school), less if packaged.

- **Explain Everything (www.explaineverything.com):** This $2.99 app uses text, video, pictures, and voice to present whatever you ask students to create.

- **IXL (www.ixl.com/math/):** This online site features adaptive individualized math through gameplay including data and graphing problems. This gives students immediate feedback and covers many skills, despite its emphasis on drills. Levels range from pre-kindergarten to eighth grade. Class price is $199/year.

- **Starfall (www.starfall.com):** This free website has a few clever activities for early literacy and math exploration, but the pay site More.Starfall has a full range of activities with a price of $70 to $270/year.

- **XtraMath (www.xtramath.org):** A free site that lets you practice math facts. It keeps track of student progress, it's easy to pick what you want your students to work on, and it's easy for kids to use it independently.

- **PrimaryGames (www.primarygames.com/math.php), Coolmath-Games (www.coolmath-games.com), SoftSchools (www.softschools.com),** and **Sheppard Software (http://tinyurl.com/ccrxoa)** are among several sites that have free math games covering all math topics at each grade level. However, they have ads, are not able to keep track of a student's success rate, and are not generally self-adaptive to the student's own skill level.

APPS FOR MATH

- **Math Blaster HyperBlast (http://tinyurl.com/q3ff7vg):** The classic game many teachers used when they were students is now updated. Cost is $0.99 to $1.99.

- **Pet Bingo (http://tinyurl.com/nceqqko):** This app is adaptable to individual's level and will have students practicing math facts, measurement, and geometry while enjoying it with their very own pet. There is progress monitoring. Price for the app $1.99.

- **Geoboard (http://tinyurl.com/kzyxjv7):** This app is the digital recreation of a geoboard. The app is simple to use, and the geometry activities are open-ended and endless. The app is free.

- **Pattern Shapes (http://tinyurl.com/nbl5osu):** Exploring geometry is what this free website is all about. Students can drag shapes to learn area, symmetry, fractions, and much more. Write equations and line of symmetry right on the screen. There is also an app, which is free.

- **Swipea Tangram Puzzles for Kids (http://tinyurl.com/nsnoazj):** This is a digital version of tangrams where students can manipulate, flip, and rotate shapes to create different pictures. App is free. Full upgrade is $0.99.

- **Thinking Blocks (http://tinyurl.com/3c6eoa):** This is a free website with manipulatives that lets students model, solve word problems, and practice with fractions.

There are many sites that allow you to use mathematical tools, such as a graphing calculator. Another option is to use software that comes with your whiteboard, which typically has all sorts of math tools built in, such as protractors, rulers, and grids.

WEBSITES FOR GRAPHING

- **SoftSchools: (www.softschools.com):** This is one of several sites that have free math games that cover all math topics at each grade, but they have ads, are not able to keep track of a student's success rate, and are not generally self-adaptive to the student's own skill level.

- **IXL (www.ixl.com/math):** This online site features adaptive individualized math through gameplay including data and graphing problems. This gives students immediate feedback and covers many skills, despite its emphasis on drills. Levels from pre-kindergarten to eighth grade. Class price is $199/year.

- **ClassTools (ClassTools.net):** A free site you can use to make graphs and charts.

- **Create-a-Graph (http://tinyurl.com/yoedjn):** Create bar, line, area, pie, and XY graphs with this free website. Easy to use, and you can print, save, or email your completed graphs.

- **RealtimeBoard (www.realtimeboard.com):** This endless whiteboard allows you to enhance your classroom lessons, create school projects, work collaboratively with team members, and so much more. There is a free education version, when you use a school email address. Upgrades are also available.

APPS FOR GRAPHING

- **The Graph Club 2.0 (http://bit.ly/1nmvNe6):** This program really helps students visualize how charts and graphs compare, and it's extremely easy to use. The program includes ready-made activities in all subject areas, including rubrics and sample graphs. District purchasing is available. Contact a representative on the site for specific prices.

- **Gliffy (www.gliffy.com):** Create professional-quality flowcharts, wireframes, diagrams, and more. Free for limited use. Upgrades available for a fee.

Many studies in recent years have shown how math games can increase student learning. In addition, a survey (http://tinyurl.com/pqms3nj) released in late summer 2014 from the Games and Learning Publishing Council indicates that the use of digital games in the classroom is becoming more popular with teachers. According to the survey, 55% of teachers who responded have students play digital games in their classroom weekly.

With this in mind, pick a math unit of study. You may wish to first research a math topic and find videos to show as an introduction. Videos from **BrainPOP (www. brainpop.com)**, **Khan Academy (www.khanacademy.org)**, and **SchoolTube (www. schooltube.com)** are just a few good sources we have found. These videos are also a great resource for guided math stations or learning centers in your classroom. See **our website (http://tinyurl.com/oexfhcv)**.

Literacy Lessons

Cross-curriculum planning is encouraged with the common core by using ELA standards in history, science, and technical subjects. Getting through all of the standards you need in third grade is very difficult in the time given. The key to planning with the CCSS is to teach multiple standards in one lesson, when you can. We hope that the following list of a few sample lessons for third grade will inspire you to become an effective technology lesson planner.

QR CODE ACTIVITY

Scan and/or take pictures from nonfiction books that focus on a subject you are studying in social studies or science. Pictures can be mounted on a large piece of construction paper. Link the poster through a QR code reader like **i-nigma Reader (www.i-nigma.com/i-nigmahp.html)** or **QR Code Generator (www.qr-code-generator. com)** to a web-based document that contains facts about the concepts that go with each picture. This primarily satisfies **W.3.6**, "with guidance and support from adults, use technology to produce and publish writing. . . ." This also satisfies **SL.3.2**, which determines the main ideas and supporting details in writing using diverse media formats. In addition, if you have students use these posters to review new information in a unit, it satisfies **W.3.8**, to "gather information from print and digital sources."

IMOVIE TRAILER

Coaches in our former building worked with third grade teachers to help with this lesson, because a little prep is needed before you begin. Start with a Google search for student iMovie Trailer examples. There are some good examples on YouTube. However, you will want to preview these iMovie Trailers before showing them to your students. Begin the lesson with a discussion about the last movie trailers students have seen. Continue by discussing what makes a good trailer. For example, they capture the interest of the audience, they do not reveal the ending, and their music reflects the mood of the movie. After viewing several examples, allow students to discuss what made those trailers interesting for them.

Next, talk about important literary elements and how these elements can be included in a movie trailer. Elements include the following.

- Readable text

- Clear recordings

- Interesting, clear images

- Timing of images

- Concise language

- Music that reflects the mood

- Narration that is louder than the background music

- Enough detail to be interesting but not enough to give away the ending

- A question or scene at the end that makes the audience want to read the book

Third grade teachers we worked with chose to do this project with a book they were reading in class. However, you can also have students use a self-selected book they are reading independently, because movie trailers make an excellent alternative to book reports. Let the students know your expectations for the completed project. For example, have students:

- Introduce the book: Include the title, the author's name, and the genre.

- Tell about the book: Introduce the main characters and action. Don't try to tell every detail.

- Tell about a favorite part of the book or make a connection: Persuade the audience to read the book and leave them wanting to know more. For example, explain what the main character has to overcome, but don't tell whether he/she is successful.

- Give a recommendation: Provide closure for the book trailer. This helps match the perfect reader for the book.

- Keep it short and sweet.

If students work together collaboratively, **W.3.6** will be satisfied, using technology, including the internet, to produce and publish writing. In the beginning, you may find your students need to plan and organize for their trailer. Apple's iMovie for Mac site (see **our website, http://tinyurl.com/oexfhcv**) has more than 29 free templates to help students work through their trailers. Students may need adult supervision and help when the time comes to scan, upload, or download pictures for their trailer. Certainly, students can provide their own illustrations and graphics, either by hand or digitally using any graphic art program (such as Microsoft Draw or Google Draw). If their book has pictures, students can scan and use them for trailers. Or, students can also search the internet to find pictures to use. Once all trailers are complete, students can share their iMovie Trailers with the class.

Finished projects can also be saved to the class ebook shelf for students to explore throughout the year. In addition to **W.3.6**, other standards satisfied include **SL.3.5**, as students are using technology to clarify information in their presentations. **SL.3.2** is also satisfied, because students are interpreting information using a diverse media format all to develop a coherent understanding of a topic (their novel or book). **W.3.8** is also satisfied, as students will need help, support, and guidance with finding and downloading images for their trailers.

Science/Social Studies Lessons

The following sample lessons address CCSS ELA standards and teach lessons based on national standards in social studies and science.

ECOSYSTEM RELATIONSHIPS

Third grade classrooms across the country study interdependent relationships in ecosystems. The following activity has students create a set of weather and climate trading cards using Wixie. Students make at least one trading card for each season, which must include a typical weather condition for that season (monsoon–summer, blizzard–winter, tornado–spring, and hurricane–fall, etc.). Each card must include the definition of the weather event, as well as describe conditions that cause the event. Students must make one trading card for climate and one trading card for weather. Students must include the definition of weather and climate and information on how they differ. One trading card will also be made for the water cycle, including the name of each part of the cycle in the order they occur. When students have finished, they should have seven trading cards. They may make additional cards that might include other weather vocabulary students have been using. Students could also record themselves on the Wixie app, narrating their trading cards. If you prefer to use something a little more authentic, ReadWriteThink's Trading Card app is a great alternative. Students follow the same procedure outlined earlier. This app allows trading cards to be printed and cut out and "traded" with students within the classroom or perhaps another classroom. With students getting to know and use various text features to locate key facts or information in a text efficiently, specifically with their research, this lesson satisfies **RI.3.5**. This activity also satisfies **RL.3.8**. Working on their trading cards, whether on Wixie or the trading card app, would then satisfy **W.3.6**. Interaction and collaborating with others will come later as students trade and discuss their trading cards. **SL.3.2** is also satisfied with this activity. Even though students are not creating a story or poem, they are creating facts for their trading cards, specifically if they narrate their Wixie trading cards. Therefore, this activity would also satisfy **SL.3.5**.

IMPORTANT LEADERS

Another lesson that third grade classrooms across the country study focuses on important people (past and present) who helped shape our nation, state, and community. With your class, brainstorm a list of leaders. Stay away from obvious choices (George Washington, Abraham Lincoln, etc.). Instead, steer students toward choices such as important Native Americans from your area, local community leaders, or national leaders, as students may not know much about Supreme Court justices, Secretary of State, etc.

Break your students into groups of four (if you have a group of three, that is fine). Name each table. For example, you may want to do something fun and name each table after a type of candy or popular destinations. This is an important component so students can keep track of the tables they have visited. From your groups, pick a table host. The table host will be the leader and does not move when the groups switch. The table host is also the person in charge of writing down the words, descriptions, and brief phrases the group brainstorms. Arrange desks/tables to accommodate the number of groups you have.

In the center of the area is an iPad. Using any of the mind-mapping sources we mentioned earlier, place a name in the center of the mind-map (making sure each group has a different name). Using the **World Café Method (http://bit.ly/1WN4w0Y)**, students will have 5 to 20 minutes to brainstorm anything they know about the person in the center of their map. The timing and how much time you can devote to this activity is up to you, keeping in mind that students need to rotate to all groups.

At the end of the allotted time, the table host thanks the group and holds up the table picture as the teacher announces the groups switch. Students are reminded that they must go to every table and cannot repeat a table. The new group gets the allotted time to go over what the previous group wrote and brainstorm new ideas about the person, as the table host records their thoughts. This process is repeated until all groups have gone to all tables. Make sure the mind-map for each table is saved, as students will need to refer to these. Repeat this process another day, if you wish, with more names.

Next, students will select a leader from the original list (which you have modified if necessary) whom they would like to research and report on. You may want to review the techniques we outlined earlier for having students search on the internet, as well as using search engines.

Before students begin their note taking, you may wish to guide them with some essential questions to include in their research. For example: Who is this person?

How have they contributed to our community? What qualities makes this person an important member of our community?

Using tools such as **Kids Click (www.kidsclick.org)** or **Google for Kids (www.safe-searchkids.com)**, students can search for information they need to complete the assignment. Make sure they stop to consult reference materials for definitions or pronunciations of words they do not know. This lesson would very easily satisfy **RI.3.5** and **W.3.8**; instructing students on how to take notes and then having them take notes on information gathered will be very helpful in writing their rough draft and eventually their project.

There are so many wonderful ways students can present their writing using technology. It is also important to mention that this project can definitely be differentiated for your classroom. Consider using Trading Cards, where students can write short text on cards and add pictures. Options requiring a little more text are Evernote, PowerPoint, Google Docs, or WikiSpaces. Students present key ideas from their research and import pictures to illustrate their points. iMovie, iMovie Trailer, Prezi, Wixie, or Pixie are other more in-depth ways for students to present what they have learned. Backgrounds and music can be added. Pictures can be scanned or imported to enhance their writing.

Students may need some guidance and support from adults to produce, publish, and share their writing projects; thus this activity also satisfies **W.3.6**. Depending on which tool the students choose to use for producing their work, both **SL.3.2** and **SL.3.5** may also be satisfied, as well as **L3.4d**.

Math Lessons

The following lesson ideas satisfy the math standard **MP5**.

AREA AND PERIMETER ACTIVITY

The third grade team at our former school had students involved in a unique math investigation for area and perimeter. Marilyn Burns, founder of **Math Solutions (www.mathsolutions.com)** and one of today's most highly respected mathematics educators, originally designed this math activity, but we updated it to include technology. Students read the book Spaghetti and Meatballs for All. Or, you can find a link for the story online. The third grade teachers sent everyone a Google Doc with the task, directions, and story link. Students then used their tablets and earbuds to listen to the story. Afterwards, students received the following task.

There are 32 people coming to dinner. Other than the arrangement that Mrs. (insert any name here) designed, please arrange the seating in as many different ways as you can to seat 32 people. In other words, arrange the seating in ways that will have a perimeter of 32. You can use apps such as Pattern Shapes to drag tiles to form arrangements, or you can use grid paper or **online grid paper (www.incompetech. com/graphpaper)**. You can change the area as much as you want. You can use more than eight tiles as long as each of your arrangements has a perimeter of 32. You can put as many tables together or keep as many separate, as you want, as long as the perimeter is 32.

Student directions are then to record each new way on the centimeter square grid paper. There are also links for interactive grid paper websites, where students can do their work. See the appendix or **our website (http://tinyurl.com/oexfhcv)**.

First students should highlight the key words and important information in the task. Next, they solve the problem on the centimeter grid paper. Students need to make sure they label their thinking, so that another person can follow along easily. Once a student has come up with as many arrangements as possible, have them choose one arrangement and explain (using Explain Everything) how they know the arrangement will work, using good math vocabulary (perimeter, area, square centimeters, etc.). This lesson covers the **MP5** by using digital tools to enhance math learning. Even though students are not creating stories or poems, they are creating explanations for their seating arrangements and must be able to explain using the appropriate math vocabulary for this lesson. Therefore, this activity also satisfies **SL.3.5**. **W.3.6** is satisfied as well, because students are using the app Explain Everything to produce and publish their mathematical thinking, reasoning, and problem solving for this task.

MULTIPLICATION STRATEGIES

The following lesson appeared in first grade and was also adapted for third grade, after a former colleague of ours heard about it. As third grade teachers begin to teach multiplication strategies, each student will make a page for the class multiplication ebook. Using your favorite media publishing tool (Wixie, eBook, iBook Author, etc.), students can pair up to write and illustrate their favorite multiplication strategy. There will be duplicates—that is OK, because every illustration and explanation is different. Students are encouraged to make their own drawings to go along with their strategy. However, they may need adult help to locate and download a picture (such as arrays or grids) from the internet.

Some suggestions for students are to:

- Show the problem in an array, a set that shows equal groups in rows and columns

- Show the problem in a grid

- Write the problem and use skip counting

- Write the problem and use repeated addition

Each page should include a heading for the strategy. As a class, making a table of contents as well as a glossary will help students learn and apply text features to math and thus satisfy **RI.3.5**. Finished books should be shared with the class, placed on a class ebook shelf, or shared with each student in their electronic math folder. Using this ebook at the beginning of the year as you introduce and work through the multiplication tables is a great way to help your students with their facts (especially the more difficult ones). Making a similar book with division strategies is an awesome way to ensure that your students are learning multiplication and division strategies all year. Students should also be encouraged, as they learn and/or find new strategies, to add them to the electronic addition and subtraction books. This activity satisfies **W.3.6**, to produce and publish writing, including collaboration with peers. Furthermore, **SL.3.5** will be addressed, as students are adding their digital photos (visual displays) to descriptions of their addition or subtraction strategies. This would also cover the **MP5** by using digital tools to enhance mathematical learning. Projecting the book as well as having a class discussion where students are answering questions about the material presented in the strategy book would satisfy **SL.3.2**.

A Final Note

It is clear that as students progress through the elementary grades, they are establishing their baseline of proficiency in technology. This will definitely enhance students' experiences with technology in middle school and high school, as well as satisfy the CCSS performance standards at the 3–5 level. There are many great ideas in this chapter that you may be able to adapt to your class. You will find more resources online at **our website (http://tinyurl.com/oexfhcv)**, which may be helpful to you and could be useful for differentiation. Please go to our online site for updated information about this book. To see grades other than 3–5, look for our three additional titles in this series.

Chapter 9

Practical Ideas for Fourth Grade

We realize that you will want to focus on your particular grade or subject when you are planning your lessons and implementing CCSS, so we have organized the practical ideas chapters by grade level, then subject. Each grade starts with an overview followed by ELA technology standards with accompanying apps, software, and websites that you can use to help your students succeed with that standard. We then continue with the math standard for the grade level, also with accompanying resources. Finally, we have included some sample lessons for each grade level in various subject areas. Although we intend for you to seek your specific grade and subject to help you implement CCSS for your students, please do not disregard other sections of this chapter. To see grades other than 3-5, look for our three additional titles in this series, as they could provide information to help you differentiate for students at all levels of your class.

The CCSS expect fourth graders to use technology to enhance their literacy skills. The literacy standards place an emphasis on information gathering and publishing of student writing. Students should also use technology to practice math skills. This includes the use of digital math tools in the form of software programs, apps, or websites. We offer ideas and suggestions for which technologies to use and how to teach with them. At the fourth grade level, students are expected to use technology with many of their literacy skills as well as possess an understanding of what technology tools are best used when solving math problems. In this chapter, we list all fourth grade standards that require teaching and learning with technology, and we have included our ideas on how to integrate technology into these standards using tablets, computers, and software, apps, or websites.

Reading Resources

There are many ways in which students can make visual and/or oral presentations of a story or drama. Using programs that help students to create the stories in a format that allows them to illustrate, as well as type, helps students with the visual presentation of the text. In many cases, these presentation programs allow students to pick backgrounds from templates and to import pictures. Most present in a slide-show format, but they can also be printed out as a storybook. Some even allow you to save presentations as ebooks. Movie creation apps, websites, and software are not conducive to stories in paragraph form; however, you can use your voice to speak the text and use photos and video to illustrate in an animated format. We have also included apps and websites that allow students to create shorter versions of their stories in an animated way. Although not as inclusive, they can be a lot of fun!

Reading Literature

RL.4.7	READING LITERATURE

Make connections between the text of a story or drama and a **visual or oral presentation** of the text, identifying where each version reflects specific descriptions and directions in the text.

THE CCSS STANDARDS FOR READING ARE designed to help ensure that students gain adequate exposure to a range of texts and tasks. Rigor is also infused through the requirement that students read increasingly complex texts through the grades and make connections between text and visual or oral presentations. Following are lists of student-friendly tools that will allow them to transform text into slideshows, books, animations, and movies.

SLIDESHOW SOFTWARE

Slideshows, which are easy to use, are a great way for students to demonstrate their understanding and share ideas with the class. The following slideshow tools can get them started.

- **Kid Pix (www.kidpix.com):** This software is not free, but students can use it to publish collaborative writing that uses pictures and text. A new version called **Kid Pix 3D** features more animation.

- **Wixie (Wixie.com) and Pixie (www.tech4learning.com/pixie):** This software for purchase uses multimedia, pictures, sound video, and text, to create presentations and stories stored on the cloud for mobile access. The apps are free, but there is an online version for schools with more features that has educational pricing.

- **Smilebox: (www.smilebox.com):** A free program linked to the website to create slideshows, invitations, greetings, collages, scrapbooks, and photo albums right on your computer. Don't miss applying for the free Teacher's Toolbox!

WEBSITES FOR BOOK CREATION

Following are some free sites that also allow you to add pictures to your text and create ebooks or printed versions.

- **Storybird (www.storybird.com):** This free website uses art to inspire storytelling to write, read, share, and print short books.

- **StoryJumper (StoryJumper.com):** This free site ($24.95 for hardbound book) gives your students a fun set of tools for writing and illustrating kid's stories that can be shared online.

- **Little Bird Tales (www.littlebirdtales.com):** This website is free. Students can draw original artwork or import pictures to create and write stories. To download work as a digital movie costs 99 cents; however, you can print stories out free.

APPS FOR STORY ANIMATION

Some apps allow students to create shorter versions of their stories in an animated way. Following are some of our recommendations.

- **Puppet Pals (http://tinyurl.com/qbgaks2):** This app allows students to create a puppet production using familiar characters to tell or retell a story. It is free, but for $2.99 you can get all the add-ons.

- **iFunFace (www.ifunface.com):** Students can create a read-aloud to show how the main idea and details flow by using a photo and audio recording to create an animation. It helps students visualize how to support details that branch off from the main ideas and how they all flow together. App is free but can be upgraded for $1.99.

- **Blabberize: (www.blabberize.com)** You can use your voice to speak the text, and photos can be used to illustrate in an animated format. Free.

- **Voki (www.voki.com):** Your voice speaks the text, and photos can be used to illustrate in an animated format. It is free, but there are ads.

- **Fotobabble (www.fotobabble.com):** You can use your voice to speak the text, and photos can be used to illustrate. Free.

MOVIE CREATION APPS, WEBSITES AND SOFTWARE

Creating movies, although more time consuming, is a fun and interactive way to present information.

- **iMovie and iMovie Trailer (www.apple.com/ios/imovie):** These are great programs to use when creating stories. iMovie Trailer has templates that make the program faster and easier to use. iMovie has many great features. These programs come free with Apple computers; however, you can also buy the app for $4.99.

- **MovieMaker (http://tinyurl.com/mnabm7):** Microsoft's version of iMovie. It comes standard with any Windows computer.

- **Animoto (www.animoto.com):** This site allows you to create professional movies, and it is free to educators.

- **Wideo (wideo.co) (not .com):** Wideo allows you to easily make animation videos. Education pricing is 75 cents per month.

- **Stupeflix: (https://studio.stupeflix.com/en/):** Make free movies using your photos and videos for up to 20 minutes. It's very easy and super fun!

Reading Information

RI.4.7	READING INFORMATION

Interpret information presented visually, orally, or quantitatively (e.g., in charts, graphs, diagrams, time lines, **animations, or interactive elements on Web pages**) and explain how the information contributes to an understanding of the text in which it appears.

YOU CAN FIND MANY INTERNET WEBSITES that show charts, graphs, diagrams, timelines, and interactive animations. Picking a topic from your science standards and finding websites on this information is a great way to integrate technology. You can then discuss all of the ways people depict information on websites.

SOFTWARE AND WEBSITES TO CREATE CHARTS AND GRAPHS

There are several software programs and websites (some must be purchased, others are free) that students can use to create their own charts and graphs. We have listed some of them here.

- **Microsoft Excel (office.com), Apple Numbers (www.apple.com/mac/numbers),** or **Google Sheets (www.google.com/sheets/about):** Use of these programs is great approache to teaching students about charts and graphs. Making charts and graphs is an excellent way to learn how to interpret and present information.

- **The Graph Club 2.0 (http://bit.ly/1nmvNe6):** This program really helps students visualize how charts and graphs compare, and it's extremely easy to use. The program includes ready-made activities in all subject areas, including rubrics and sample graphs. District purchasing and volume CDs are available. Contact a representative on the site for specific prices.

- **Gliffy (www.gliffy.com):** Create professional-quality flowcharts, wireframes, diagrams, and more. Limited use is free. Upgrades available for a fee.

- **Create-a-Graph (http://tinyurl.com/yoedjn):** Create bar, line, area, pie, and XY graphs with this free website. Easy to use, and you can print, save, or email your completed graphs.

- **ClassTools (classtools.net):** Create graphs and charts (along with lots of other useful classroom tools like a QR code generator or timeline!) with this free website.

- **ChartGizmo (chartgizmo.com):** With your free account from ChartGizmo you can start creating dynamic charts from static or collected data and place them on your website in minutes.

SOFTWARE AND WEBSITES TO CREATE TIMELINES

Students can make the connections between time and events visually. This can be difficult because it requires abstract thinking. Use a topic from your literacy social studies standards to integrate this standard (**RL4.7**) using timelines and interactive elements, such as pictures and videos, into your curriculum.

- **Timeliner (http://tinyurl.com/556cvc):** Organize any sequential information on a horizontal, vertical, or circular timeline in minutes. More than 400 customizable activity files in language arts, science, and social studies are included with the program, as well as 50 ready-made research assignments that include free, educationally appropriate articles from Grolier Online. Various pricing is available.

- **SoftSchools (www.softschools.com):** Timeline Maker, which is an easy program to use and print, is included in SoftSchools' free site; however, there are ads.

- **OurStory (www.ourstory.com):** This is a collaborative timeline. You can create and share privately or publicly. It is free; however, you do need to sign up on their website.

- **ReadWriteThink (www.readwritethink.org):** A free site that has many good teacher resources, including great ways for students to make their own timelines. It is so easy to make and display them!

Writing Resources

Presenting information digitally to aid comprehension is another standard fourth graders will be expected to do. Traditionally, **Microsoft PowerPoint (office.com)** has been the presentation tool of choice. Although this is still a great program to use, other presentation programs have emerged. Apple offers **Keynote (www.apple.com/mac/keynote)** as part of their software package. Its features are very similar to PowerPoint. Another program that has emerged is **Google Slides (www.google.com/slides/about)**. It is aimed toward business use; however, it is free and web-based. It is also very easy to share. Multiple users can work on it at once, which makes this an especially great program to use when interacting and collaborating remotely. You can also add audio recordings to your slides, as well as visual displays such as pictures and short video clips. These can be used to enhance the development of main ideas or the themes of your presentations. **Evernote (evernote.com)** is a free app that also allows your students to share notes as well as audio and video recordings. It's easy to use and share with others.

Writing

W.4.2a | WRITING

Introduce a topic clearly and group related information in paragraphs and sections; include formatting (e.g., headings), illustrations, and **multimedia** when useful to aiding comprehension.

W.4.6 | WRITING

With some guidance and support from adults, use **technology, including the Internet**, to produce and publish writing as well as to interact and collaborate with others; demonstrate sufficient command of **keyboarding skills** to type a minimum of one page in a single sitting.

PRESENTING DIGITALLY IS NOT LIMITED TO slide show presentations. There are many websites out there that allow you to publish student writing. Using blogging websites, such as **Edmodo (edmodo.com)** and **Wikispaces (wikispaces.com)** is another way to share student writing in a safe, protected environment. It is also a great way for students to interact and collaborate with others. Both of these sites allow teachers to set themselves up as administrators and add students to different groups. All student writing is secure in these groups.

WEBSITES TO PUBLISH WRITING

You can give assignments that ask all students to provide short answers, or you can give longer written assignments to individual students. They can then work on their writing and submit privately to you, or post on a website to share. There are also sites that ask students to submit their work for possible publication online. The following are a few of our recommendations.

- **PBS Kids Writing (pbskids.org/writerscontest):** This free site asks for student writing and serves as a nice incentive to get students to do their best writing.

- **Lulu (www.lulu.com) and Lulu Jr (www.lulujr.com):** These sites allow you to create real books and publish them online. Parents can purchase the books as a keepsake. The site is free to use, but a fee is required to publish.

- **TikaTok (www.tikatok.com):** This is another site that allows students to write, create, and publish stories as ebooks or hardcover books. **TikaTok Story Spark** is an app that you can purchase for $3. Classroom price for TikaTok starts at $19 a year.

- **Cast UDL Book Builder (http://bookbuilder.cast.org):** This free site lets you publish your ebook and see what others have published.

- **Poetry Idea Engine from Scholastic (http://tinyurl.com/2cuowf):** This is a site that allows you to use templates to make different forms of poetry. This is an example of another great way technology gets kids writing—and it is free!

KEYBOARDING SOFTWARE

By fourth grade, students are expected to type a page in one sitting. There are lots of keyboarding programs that you can buy. The following are some tried and true programs that we have used.

- **Mavis Beacon Keyboarding Kidz (http://tinyurl.com/254v9on):** This program allows you to set your own words-per-minute goals, see what keys you need to practice, and see what keys you know well. Play games to practice what you've learned and to improve your speed and accuracy. ($19.99)

- **Type to Learn (http://ttl4.sunburst.com):** This typing program, for Grades K–12, emphasizes both accuracy and words-per-minute speed, and it provides each student with individualized remediation and goals for success. Consult the website for various pricing options and to request a quote.

- **Typing Training (www.typingtraining.com):** This web-based program with apps (for Grades 3–12) allows access from any computer or handheld device. Animated coaches are available with a customizable curriculum. Students can play games or choose from more than 2,500 unique exercises while tracking progress with detailed reports and graphs. Consult the website for various options and to request a quote.

KEYBOARDING WEBSITES

Paying for a good typing program is worth the expense. A quality program keeps track of student progress and their levels of accomplishment. If you can't buy a program, following are free sites that offer some instruction and games.

- **TypingWeb (www.typing.com):** This site does have ads, but it does keep track of student progress with typing skills and allows reports. Free.

- **TypeRacer (play.typeracer.com):** Free website where you can race opponents by typing words in paragraph form. For experienced typists to bone up on accuracy and typing speed. There are ads.

Some districts have students go to computer labs to practice keyboarding at given times, others fit it in where they can in the classroom, and still others have students practice and learn at home. We have found that the best way is to combine all three. Students benefit from formal keyboarding instruction, but they need to practice both in the classroom and at home. When students are working at the computers in your classroom, they need repeated reminders to keep up good techniques such as sitting up straight, keeping hands in home row, wrists slightly curved, and moving the fingers instead of the hands.

Writing Research

W.4.8	WRITING RESEARCH
Recall relevant information from experiences or gather relevant information from print and **digital sources**; take notes and categorize information, and provide a list of sources.	

BY THE TIME STUDENTS ARE IN FOURTH GRADE, they should be able to search the internet to gather the information that they need on a given topic. Your class will need guidance, of course, so lessons on internet searching are critical, as well as lessons on media literacy. (Media literacy is especially crucial, because students now need to be able to critique a website before using it—anyone can put up a webpage.) As stated by the **W.4.8** standard, students will also need to be able to take notes off these sites and categorize their information as well as provide a list of sources. We discuss these techniques in the following paragraphs.

Although students are sufficiently net-savvy these days, they still need assistance with the basics of searching. Different search engines work in different ways, and each will give you different information. Your students need to know how to use multiple engines.

Smart searching will help avoid a lot of wasted time. Teaching students to analyze search results will definitely help them find better information and to think more critically about any information they find on the internet. Following are a few rules of thumb.

- Choose your search terms carefully. Be precise about what you are looking for, though you should use phrases and not full sentences.

- Adding more words can narrow a search. Use Boolean searches to narrow your topic with quotation marks. There's a big difference between "gopher" and

"Habitats of gophers in North America."

- Use synonyms! If students can't find what they're looking for, have them try keywords that mean the same thing or are related.

- Type "site:" Typing site: (with the colon) after your keyword and before a URL will tell Google to search within a specific website.

- Add a minus sign. Adding a minus sign (a hyphen) immediately before any word, with no space in between, indicates that you don't want that word to appear in your search results. For example, "Saturn -cars" will give you information about the planet, not the automobile.

KID-FRIENDLY SEARCH ENGINES

Browsing safe content is the most important reason for using search engines made specifically for kids. Allowing your students to have the run of the web using a search engine for kids helps you, because it is difficult to monitor many students at once if your class is using adult search engines.

There is no guarantee that every search will be kid-safe; however, the following search engines are specifically for young children.

- **Kids Click (www.kidsclick.org):** This is a web search site designed for kids by librarians. This site is free and for Grades 2-5.

- **Google for Kids (www.safesearchkids.com):** Google for Kids Safe Search Kids is a custom search engine using Google's Safe Search features with additional filtering to block more potentially harmful material than if you simply use Google. It is fun, colorful, and easy for students to use.

- **Google Kid Search (www.kidzsearch.com):** This is another safe search engine powered by Google for Grades K-8. However, please be aware that there are ads on this site.

- **Yahoo for Kids (http://tinyurl.com/nqn4p39):** Yahooligans is a safe search engine for young students picked by editors at Yahoo.

- **Ask Kids (www.ask.com):** This is a free, filtered search engine for Grades K-6.

Tried and true methods for taking notes and categorizing information from books can still be used to gather information and take notes on websites. Teaching students to use data sheets, note cards, and KWL (Know, What, Learn) techniques still works; however, there are now ways that technology can help and sometimes make it easier. Apps such as Evernote, are a great way to take notes. The **Kentucky Virtual**

Library (http://tinyurl.com/ptnwz4) is a fine website to use as a resource for some of these techniques.

Modeling is of course essential when teaching students how to glean information from a website. An interactive whiteboard is a perfect tool to use during your modeling lesson. Don't have an interactive whiteboard? Use **RealtimeBoard (www.realtimeboard.com)**. It's a free website that allows you to turn an ordinary whiteboard into an interactive one. All you need is a computer and a projector to use this virtual whiteboard. Using the many tools an interactive whiteboard and software have to offer will really help teach your students how to navigate through information posted on the internet.

MIND-MAPPING TOOLS

Mind-mapping tools will help your students organize their research when gathering information. Several wonderful software programs have been used for mind-mapping for many years. However, there are also free sites out there. Following are some digital tools you can use to teach note taking and categorizing.

- **Kidspiration (http://tinyurl.com/dg2cxa):** This is a mind-mapping software program that helps students organize their writing. It can be especially helpful for students who are learning to create paragraphs and organize big ideas into smaller parts. Cost is $40 to $640. The web-based version is called **Webspiration (http://tinyurl.com/bmop3nh)** and costs $6/month.

- **Bubbl.us (Bubbl.us):** This is a free (with limited use) mind-mapping website for Grades K–12. It can be shared by multiple students at a time and comes with an app. For more options, purchase a package for $6/month or $59/year. Both come with a 30-day free trial. Site licensing is available. Contact the company for specifics.

- **Mindmeister (www.mindmeister.com/education):** This is a free, basic, mind-mapping website for Grades 2–12. Upgrades are available. Educational pricing is available for schools and universities (e.g., $6 per user for 6 months with 20+ users). All of the upgrades have a free trial period.

- **FreeMind (http://tinyurl.com/5qrd5):** This is a free mind-mapping tool for Grades 2–12. Options for a basic or maximum install are available.

- **ClassTools (www.classtools.net):** Organize ideas with this free collection of tools, games, quizzes, and diagrams.

Fourth graders will also need to provide a list of sources. Of course, making your own template for sources and having the students fill it in using a word processing program works; however, there are websites, such as **EasyBib (www.easybib.com)**, that students can use to generate citations in MLA, APA, and Chicago formats easily. EasyBib is a free website and app for ages 5–12. Simply copy and paste or scan a book's barcode to create its citation. Students can also cite a list of sources on their own by including URL, publisher or author, topic/title, and date a website was published. If the date published is not available, they should note the date retrieved from the internet.

Media Literacy Resources

Your class also needs to be aware that links come up in searches that may have strings attached—not to the research topic, but to advertisers. This should be a part of your media literacy lesson. Students can waste a great deal of time if they don't realize what it is they are looking for. Students also need to know that anyone can put up a website, and they need to know how to tell whether a site is credible. Determining whether a site is a .com (stands for company), .gov (a government site), or .org (a non-profit organization, such as a school) is the first step. Then students need to see who the author of the site is (this will usually be posted at the beginning or the end), who they are affiliated with, or what is the author's background or expertise on the topic. Your students will also need to know that advertisers abound, and students will need to be careful what they click on. The class needs to be taught what to do if they go to an inappropriate site (such as hitting the back button immediately and letting a teacher know). The website **Joe Cool/Joe Fool: (http://tinyurl.com/pojhuuw)** is a good site to use. It provides online media literacy lessons complete with quizzes.

Speaking and Listening

> **SL.4.2** | SPEAKING AND LISTENING
>
> Paraphrase portions of a text read aloud or information presented in **diverse media and formats**, including visually, quantitatively, and orally.

> **SL.4.5** | SPEAKING AND LISTENING
>
> Add **audio recordings and visual displays** to presentations when appropriate to enhance the development of main ideas or themes.

THERE ARE MANY MEDIA FORMATS that allow text to be read aloud. Audio books on CD or ebooks are great sources to use. Sites such as **Follett Shelf (http://tinyurl.com/oux56og)** and **TumbleBooks (TumbleBooks.com)** (must be purchased) allow you to have access to multiple ebooks, which include fiction as well as nonfiction. You can also check out many ebooks at your local library or purchase them from booksellers, such as Amazon or Barnes & Noble (especially if you have e-readers). There are some free ebooks out there. Of course, sites that you pay for give you a much better selection. Using ebooks or a website with your interactive whiteboard (or free whiteboard sites) allows interaction when modeling or for student engagement. Informational text works especially well with this standard; however, fictional pieces can also be used.

APPS FOR PARAPHRASING

After listening to text read aloud, students can use different media formats to paraphrase what they heard. Because you are paraphrasing and keeping it short, you can use these fun, interactive apps.

- **Comic Life (http://tinyurl.com/oj5o2qd):** Make a comic from your own images with fonts, templates, panels, balloons, captions, and lettering art. This tool in available as software or as an app at various pricing.

- **ToonDoo (toondoo.com):** Create your own comics to upload online, or create a comic storybook. The app is free; however, you can also purchase printable images or ToonDooSpaces.

- **Puppet Pals (http://tinyurl.com/qbgaks2):** This app allows students to create a puppet production using familiar characters to tell or retell a story. It is free, but for $2.99 you can get all the add-ons.

- **iFunFace (www.ifunface):** Students can create a read-aloud to show how the main idea and details flow by using a photo and audio recording to create an animation. It helps students visualize how to support details that branch off from the main ideas and how they all flow together. The app is free but can be upgraded for $1.99.

APPS AND WEBSITES FOR PRESENTATIONS

Scanning finished book pages into Microsoft PowerPoint, Apple Keynote, or Google Slides allow you to make ebooks or presentations for your classroom by adding audio recordings and visual displays to enhance the development of main ideas or themes as stated in **SL.4.5**. These programs allow you to speak directly into the program, and then easily store the ebooks for all students. Options include controlling the speed of page advancement, recording narration, adding action buttons, adjusting mouse over and mouse click actions, incorporating preset animation, and setting page transition effects. Following are resources that students can use to share work and create presentations.

- **Cast UDL Bookbuilder (http://bookbuilder.cast.org):** This free site allows students to create and share their own ebooks online. You can also read what other students have written there.

- **Prezi (www.prezi.com):** You can sign up for a free educational account, and your students can create and share presentations online. Prezi has mind-mapping, zoom, and motion and can import files. Presentations can be downloaded. A Prezi viewer app is available.

- **WebQuests (www.webquest.org):** These are good tools to use for presenting main ideas or themes. WebQuest is a website that allows students to follow a project-based lesson where information is found solely on the internet. You can also create your own WebQuest if you have a website building program or a website such as **Kafafa (www.kafafa.com/kafafa)**. WebQuest.org is the original and most popular site; however, if you search the internet, you will find more sites that you can use.

Language Resources

Merriam-Webster (www.merriam-webster.com) is still the most commonly used digital dictionary and thesaurus. They also offer a kid-friendly version of this dictionary called **Word Central (www.wordcentral.com)**. This resource includes the pronunciation of the word as well as its definition. The original Merriam-Webster site has this as well, and includes multiple definitions. Kids. **WordsmythKids**

(www./kids.wordsmyth.net/we) and **WordSmyth (www.wordsmyth.net)** are good fourth grade options. The kids' version includes pronunciation (as does the adults') and shows how words are used as a part of speech with examples and pictures if applicable. **Little Explorers (http://tinyurl.com/2swjc)** is another good option for a dictionary and thesauruses, and it includes a glossary maker. You can sign up for an ad-free version, which will not cost your school. **Thesaurus.com** is a great thesaurus site. While digital dictionaries and thesauruses are not updated as often as encyclopedias, they are still very convenient to use and are kept relatively current. These sites should be bookmarked or put on your website for easy access. The more students use them, the more comfortable they will become. You should offer lessons and activities to learn and practice the necessary skills with an online dictionary, just as you would when using hard-copy dictionaries, glossaries, and thesauruses.

Language

> **L.4.4c** | LANGUAGE
>
> Consult reference materials (e.g., dictionaries, glossaries, thesauruses), both print and **digital**, to find the pronunciation and determine or clarify the precise meaning of key words and phrases.

ONE LESSON IDEA IS TO HAVE STUDENTS locate difficult vocabulary words in a piece of informational text and then use an electronic dictionary to define them. You could give students a website to read (preferably on a standards topic from literacy or science) and ask them to write down all of the words they don't know. After using an electronic dictionary to find the definitions to these words, have students reread the text. With luck, they will come away with a better understanding of the content they read.

Using the app or website **Trading Cards (http://tinyurl.com/8lqftek)** is a great way to document vocabulary words by adding their definitions, a picture, and recordings of pronunciation. You can also use Trading Cards by doing an activity with an online thesaurus. You can give a student a word on a trading card, and then ask them to make as many trading cards as they can of synonyms and antonyms of that word. You can print these out and trade them with others or make them into a digital book. The app Explain Everything is also easy to use to import a picture, record your voice, and make a digital presentation.

Math Resources

THERE ARE TWO MAIN SETS OF BENCHMARKS—processes and practices—in the Common Core Math standards. First, you have the math targets, written similarly to ELA (Counting and Cardinality; Operations & Algebraic Thinking; Number & Operation in Base Ten; Measurement & Data; and Geometry). While you work with students on mathematical processes like algebra and fractions in fourth grade, you need to teach your students how to apply the Standards for Mathematical Practices, such as problem solving and precision, to those processes. One practice, the only one that includes technology, is mathematical practice 5, "Use appropriate tools strategically."

MP5	MATH
Use appropriate **tools** strategically.	

Following is the explanation CCSS provides for **MP5**. As this is the standard explanation for grade K-12, it does include references to higher grades.

> Mathematically proficient students consider the available tools when solving a mathematical problem. These tools might include pencil and paper, concrete models, a ruler, a protractor, **a calculator, a spreadsheet, a computer algebra system, a statistical package, or dynamic geometry software**. Proficient students are sufficiently familiar with tools appropriate for their grade or course to make sound decisions about when each of these tools might be helpful, recognizing both the insight to be gained and their limitations. For example, mathematically proficient high school students analyze graphs of functions and solutions generated using a **graphing calculator**. They detect possible errors by strategically using estimation and other mathematical knowledge. When making mathematical models, they know that technology can enable them to visualize the results of varying assumptions, explore consequences, and compare predictions with data. Mathematically proficient students at various grade levels are able to identify relevant external mathematical resources, such as **digital content located on a website**, and use them to pose or solve problems. They are able to use **technological tools** to explore and deepen their understanding of concepts.

Because this description did not give examples for all grades, we have provided a list of appropriate apps, websites, and software and included lessons that will help translate this standard for fourth grade.

This is the only fourth grade math standard that involves technology. There are many math programs, websites, and apps out there. The best of them have students learning in creative ways and are not just electronic worksheets. They automatically adapt to the students' skill levels, and they give you data that tells you where students are in their learning and what they need to effectively continue. Of course, these usually do not come free. Following are many good math resources. The free resources (many with ads) are often less interesting to students and not as well organized. They don't give you the feedback you need. However, you must make the decision about what is best for your circumstances and budget.

WEBSITES FOR MATH

Here are some tools and resources that you can use to help students meet the fourth grade math standards.

- **ScootPad (www.scootpad.com):** This is a web-based math site that is totally customizable for individual students. It adapts to the student and keeps the teacher in the loop with multiple reports. It is completely aligned to the CCSS. The price for a class varies from $5 to $20/month.

- **DreamBox Learning Math (www.dreambox.com):** This individualized, adaptive game-based math resource keeps students coming back for more. It is available online or as an app. Price is $12.95/month (home) or $25/month (school), less if packaged.

- **Explain Everything (www.explaineverything.com):** This $2.99 app uses text, video, pictures, and voice to present nearly everything you ask students to create.

- **IXL (www.ixl.com/math/):** This online site features adaptive individualized math through gameplay. This gives students immediate feedback and covers many skills, despite its emphasis on drills. Levels range from pre-kindergarten to eighth grade. Class price is $199/year.

- **Starfall (www.starfall.com):** This free website has a few clever activities for early literacy and math exploration, but the pay site **More.Starfall** has a full range of activities with a price of $70 to $270/year.

- **XtraMath (www.xtramath.org):** This great site lets you practice math facts. It keeps track of student progress, it's easy to pick what you want your students to work on, and students can use it independently. And it's free!

- **PrimaryGames (www.primarygames.com/math.php), Coolmath-Games (Coolmath-Games.com), SoftSchools (SoftSchools.com),** and **Sheppard Software** (http://tinyurl.com/ccrxoa) are several sites that have free math games covering all math topics at each grade level. However, they have ads, are not able to keep track of a student's success rate, and are not generally self-adaptive to the student's own skill level.

APPS FOR MATH

There are many math apps available. The following recommendations are ideal for fourth grade students.

- **Math Blaster HyperBlast (http://tinyurl.com/q3ff7vg):** The classic game many teachers used when they were students is now updated. Cost is $0.99 to $1.99.

- **Geoboard (http://tinyurl.com/kzyxjv7):** This app is the digital recreation of a geoboard. The app is simple to use, and the geometry activities are open-ended and endless. The app is free.

- **Swipea Tangram Puzzles for Kids (http://tinyurl.com/nsnoazj):** This is a digital version of tangrams where students can manipulate, flip, and rotate shapes to create different pictures. App is free. Full upgrade is $0.99.

- **Thinking Blocks (http://tinyurl.com/3c6eoa):** The free site has manipulatives with blocks so you can model, solve word problems, and practice with fractions. Thinking Blocks is also available as a free app.

WEBSITES FOR GRAPHING

As stated in the standard, "Mathematically proficient students consider the available tools when solving a mathematical problem. These tools might include a calculator, a spreadsheet, a computer algebra system, a statistical package, or dynamic geometry software. Proficient students are sufficiently familiar with tools appropriate for their grade or course to make sound decisions about when each of these tools might be helpful, recognizing both the insight to be gained and their limitations."

The following websites allow you to use various mathematical tools, such as a graphing calculator.

- **SoftSchools (SoftSchools.com):** This is one of several sites that have free math games that cover all math topics at each grade, including a graphing section. However, they have ads, are not able to keep track of a student's success rate, and are not generally self-adaptive to the student's own skill level. Free.

- **IXL (www.ixl.com/math):** This online site features adaptive individualized math through gameplay, which includes problems related to data and graphs.

This gives students immediate feedback and covers many skills, despite its emphasis on drills. Levels range from pre-kindergarten to eighth grade. Class price is $199/year.

- **Create-a-Graph (http://tinyurl.com/yoedjn):** Create bar, line, area, pie, and XY graphs with this free website. This tool is easy to use, and you can print, save, or e-mail your completed graphs.

- **RealtimeBoard (www.realtimeboard.com):** This endless whiteboard allows you to enhance your classroom lessons, create school projects, work collaboratively with team members, and so much more. There is a free education version, when you use a school email address. Upgrades are also available.

Another option is to use software that comes with a whiteboard. These have all sorts of mathematical tools, such as protractors, rulers, and grids, built in.

APPS AND SOFTWARE FOR GRAPHING

Apps and software apps for graphing are numerous. The following two resources are good options.

- **The Graph Club 2.0 (http://bit.ly/1nmvNe6):** This program really helps students visualize how charts and graphs compare, and it's extremely easy to use. The program includes ready-made activities in all subject areas, including rubrics and sample graphs. District purchasing and volume CDs are available. Contact a representative on the site for specific prices.

- **Gliffy (www.gliffy.com):** Create professional-quality flowcharts, wireframes, diagrams, and more. Free for limited use. Upgrades are available for a fee.

In fourth grade, students are also expected to use a protractor to measure angles. They can use the app **Protractor 1st (www.skypaw.com/apps)**, which is part of the Multi Measures 2 app that includes a converter that can measure pairs of units. **Softpedia (www.softpedia.com)** is a site that allows you to download a protractor to use online. The site is free, but has ads.

Many studies in recent years have shown how math games can increase student learning. In addition, a survey (http://tinyurl.com/pqms3nj) released in late summer 2014 from the Games and Learning Publishing Council indicates that the use of digital games in the classroom is becoming more popular with teachers. According to the survey, 55% of teachers who responded have students play digital games in their classroom weekly.

With this in mind, pick a math unit of study. You may wish to first research this math topic and find videos to show as an introduction. Videos from **BrainPOP (www.brainpop.com)**, **Khan Academy (www.khanacademy.org)**, and **School Tube (www.schooltube.com)** are just a few good sources we have found. However, please be advised that you should view any video before showing it to the class. These activities are also a great way to set up guided math stations or learning centers.

Literacy Lessons

Cross-curriculum planning is encouraged with the common core by using ELA standards in history, science, and technical subjects. Getting through all of the standards you need in fourth grade is very difficult in the time given. The key to planning with the CCSS is to teach multiple standards in one lesson, when you can. We hope that the following list of sample lessons for fourth grade will inspire you to become an effective technology lesson planner.

IMMIGRATION

As coaches, we teamed with our former colleagues who taught fourth grade and designed a literacy unit on immigration. This is what they were covering in social studies. However, teachers wanted to integrate the social studies topic with literacy, writing, and technology, thus covering a myriad of standards. Using a variety of informational as well as fictional text, students read about immigration over the centuries, the hardships and obstacles they faced, their contributions, and the impact they made. Students also compared and contrasted immigrants from the past with those of today. To show knowledge, students chose from several writing prompts. Sample prompts include the following.

- Narrative: After reading multiple informational pieces and some historical fiction stories, create an imaginative narrative that describes an immigrant's journey and experience in the United States.

- Info/Explain: Write a piece that informs and explains about the different tests that immigrants needed to go through to enter the United States.

- Info/Explain: Write a piece that informs and explains the effects of immigrants on the United States. What contributions did immigrants make to the United States? How is the student's present-day life affected by the "things" that immigrants brought with them?

- Opinion: Write an opinion piece that explains which island you would rather come through, Ellis Island or Angel Island, and why.

- Opinion: Write an opinion piece that explains whether illegal immigrants should be allowed to stay in the United States or should be deported, and give your reasons.

Using tools such as **Kids Click (www.kidsclick.org)** or **Google for Kids (www.safe-searchkids.com)**, students can search for information they need to complete the assignment (making sure they stop to consult reference materials for definitions or pronunciations of words they do not know). This would very easily satisfy **W.4.8**. As we mentioned earlier, instructing students on how to take notes and then having them take notes on information gathered will be very beneficial in helping them to write their rough draft and eventually their project.

There are so many wonderful ways students can present their writing using technology. It is also important to mention that this project can definitely be differentiated for your classroom. Consider using Trading Cards, where students can write short text on cards and add pictures. Options requiring a little more text are Evernote, PowerPoint, Google Docs, or Wikispaces. Students present key ideas from their research and import pictures to illustrate their points. iMovie, iMovie Trailer, Prezi, Wixie, or Pixie are other more in depth ways for students to present what they have learned. Backgrounds and music can be added. Pictures can be scanned or imported to enhance their writing.

This interesting and in-depth activity satisfies many standards including **RI.4.7**, **RL.4.7**, and **W.4.2a**. Students may need some guidance and support from adults to produce, publish, and share their writing projects; thus this activity also satisfies **W.4.6**. Depending on which tool the students choose to use for producing their work, both **SL.4.2** and **SL.4.5** may also be satisfied, as well as **L4.4c**.

ANIMAL ADAPTATIONS

This next lesson about how animals adapt to their habitat, characteristics of animals, and animal survival nicely integrates literacy and science. We adapted it with our former fourth grade teachers after learning about it from a coach at a neighboring school. This particular lesson can also be differentiated very easily.

Once again, using a tool from earlier, such as Kidsclick or Google for Kids (or your own favorites), students search for information (making sure they stop to consult reference materials for definition or pronunciation of words they do not know). This would very easily satisfy **W.4.8**. As we mentioned earlier, instructing students on how to take notes and then having them take notes on information gathered is very beneficial.

Using Comic Life, students make a dictionary entry for an animal. Using a favorite presentation tool, such as Wixie, Keynote, iMovie, or PowerPoint, all dictionary entries can be combined and then shared through the classroom ebook shelf, Microsoft PowerPoint, Google Docs, Cast UDL Bookbuilder, and so on.

Another way students may wish to display their information is making a presentation about their habitat and the animal characteristics and survival. You may want to make a guide for your students, outlining what information must be included. For example: what kind of habitat, characteristics, and survival did you research? What animals or plants can be found in your habitat? What problems did the topic you researched have? Using your favorite presentation tool (such as Keynote, Evernote, PowerPoint, Google Slides, Wikispaces, iMovie, iMovie trailer, Wixie, or Pixie), students make a slide show displaying the information they learned about their habitat, animal characteristics, and animal survival. Student drawings can be scanned and uploaded to their presentation. Pictures from the internet (with adult supervision, of course) can also be imported and placed in the presentation to illustrate the information presented. Students can also record facts, a narrative, or music to accompany their slide show.

Students may also like to make a brochure to display the information they learned about their habitat, animal characteristics, and animal survival. Once again, you may want to make a guide for your students outlining what information must be included. The teachers we worked with created a template using any of the online brochure templates, which also included the headings listed for each section. Students also had the option to use word processing software, such as Office or Pages. The brochure can be two sided and printed as such. Students found and uploaded pictures to go with each section. Then use a reader like **i-nigma Reader (www.i-nigma.com/i-nigmahp.html)** or **QR Code Generator (www.qr-code-generator.com)**. QR codes are also added to include more information in each section. Parents loved this display in the hallway! It kept them busy reading and using their QR readers.

Many standards are satisfied with this very engaging lesson, including **RI.4.7**, **RL.4.7**, and **W.4.2a**. Students may need some guidance and support from adults to produce, publish, and share their projects; thus this activity also satisfies **W.4.6**. Depending on which tool the students choose to use for producing their work, both **SL.4.2** and **SL.4.5** may also be satisfied, as well as **L.4.4**.

Social Studies and Science Lessons

The following sample lessons address CCSS ELA standards and teach lessons based on national standards in social studies and science.

SOCIAL STUDIES REVIEW

Fourth grade teachers we previously worked with decided to try something new. The teachers worked with the reading specialist and the technology coach to come up with a plan for students to show what they know in social studies. After studying regions of the United States all year, students picked a region they would like to visit and then researched that region. Teachers made a template with Google Docs, which students then made a copy of and renamed using their name and region. Next, students chose two separate resources on the same topic (region) and entered the title/author on the research page. Taking notes in a three-column format (provided for students on the Google Docs), students researched the following big ideas: geography, resources, tourism, climate, and any other interesting facts they found. At least two supporting details were required for each source. Next, students were asked to turn their research into an opinion piece designed to convince others why their region is such a great place to visit. Once this work was done, students created an advertisement showing others why they should visit the region. Students were provided with several examples of advertisements and reflected on things they noticed in the advertisements. Next, students were given four choices, using four different tools, from which they could choose to make their advertisement.

Following are the options.

Choice 1: Sometimes you might see advertisements in magazines, on city buses, or flyers hanging around town. Comic Life is an excellent app that will allow you to use headings, text, speech bubbles, and insert fascinating photos.

Choice 2: Wixie is a tool you've probably used before and are most comfortable with. This allows you to take images, drawings, or clipart and narrate with a voice recording to make a slideshow. You cannot use video with this tool.

Choice 3: Many advertisements these days come in the form of websites. Google Sites will allow you to create your very own website where you can add as many pages as you want to promote your region. This gives you more flexibility with adding more information, pictures, videos, and links to other websites.

Choice 4: iMovie Trailers are a great way to include real images and a short amount of text. They are captivating and will allow you to keep the advertisement short and sweet. On the other hand, you may want to create a new project as an iMovie so that you can also narrate with your own voice. The choice is yours!

This intriguing activity satisfies many standards including **RI.4.7** and **W.4.2a**. Students will need some guidance and support from adults to produce, publish, and share their advertisements; thus this activity also satisfies **W.4.6**. Also, the standard **W.4.8** will be met. Depending on which tool the students choose to use for producing their work, both **SL.4.2** and **SL.4.5** may also be satisfied.

MAPPING ACTIVITIES

Another engaging lesson taught students about mapping. Using latitude and longitude as the learning target, students use a research outline to find the latitude and longitude for an assigned continent. Students need to find information such as where a continent is located (hemisphere, coordinates, etc.). Then, as a group, students choose three or four different landforms that can be found on their continent. Next, they find the coordinates of each landform and provide information about it. Finally, students choose one of the landforms they would like to visit as a group. They explain why they would like to go there and what they would do while there. After finding their information, students next make slides using the program Wixie, outlining and illustrating all of their information. One of the slides is a coordinate graph grid where students place their continent, coordinating with latitude and longitude. Students take turns narrating their pages. Finally, presentations are turned into ebooks to be shared with the class via ebook shelf. This lesson plan covers standard **RL.4.7** as well as **SL.4.5**. When students orally narrate their Wixie project, **W.4.2a** can also be satisfied with this lesson.

Math Lessons

The following two lesson ideas satisfy the **MP5** standard as well as several other ELA standards.

EXPLAIN YOUR WORK

Our colleagues who taught fourth grade were concerned about how their students might show and explain math standard **4.OA.A**, "use the four operations with whole numbers to solve problems." Teachers were looking for an innovative way for students to clearly analyze, synthesize, and explain what steps they took to solve a problem and identify which strategies they used to find their answer, including math vocabulary, in their explanation. Using a screencasting app, such as Show Me or Explain Everything, students can work on a problem, create a video (recording of their explanation) for solving the problem, and point or write on their tablets as they present to the class. This lesson covers the **MP5** standard. Even though students are not creating stories or poems, they are creating explanations, and they must be able to explain using the appropriate math vocabulary for this lesson. Therefore, this activity also satisfies **SL.4.5**. Also satisfied is **W.4.6**, as students are using the app Explain Everything to produce and publish their mathematical thinking, reasoning, and problem solving for this task.

CALIFORNIA TRIP

This next lesson is very popular with fourth grade students and teachers across the country. There are many versions out there on the internet, as well as ways to differentiate and extend this lesson. Search the web with the phrase "California Here We Come" to see alternative versions, as well as extensions to this lesson.

This lesson is perfect after teaching graphing and map reading, and when you begin the fourth grade social studies unit on states and capitals. Students work in teams to travel across the United States. Each team of students will decide which East Coast capital they will begin the race in, discuss which way they think will be the fastest, and analyze why they have made that decision. They should make sure to keep track of their decisions and rationale using any of your favorite programs, such as Wixie, Keynote, or Microsoft Word.

First, the team designs a chart or table to record the mileage from capital to capital. This can be done in a table or spreadsheet. Using MapQuest, they begin the trip. Teams travel west and must stop at the capital for each state they drive through. The route they choose is up to them, but they must record all miles traveled, as well as plot their routes onto a blank U.S. map, which has been uploaded and shared with each team. Students need to be able to draw on the map, so importing it into your favorite drawing program (Wixie, Microsoft Draw, etc.) would be beneficial. The team reaching Sacramento, California, with the fewest number of miles traveled wins!

Upon reaching Sacramento, each team will total the number of miles traveled. The students' next task is to determine how much money would be needed to buy gas for the trip (using the average of 23 miles per gallon of gas at the current price found online.) Students will resolve the problem using 60 miles an hour average and nine hours a day traveling. This will give them the number of days it would have taken to make the trip. Then students can calculate the number of days needed if they only traveled 7 hours a day averaging 60 miles an hour.

Teams also decide how much money was spent on food if breakfast cost $4.50 each, lunch cost $5.25, and supper was $7.35. Then teams need to determine how much money was spent for each night in a hotel. Students present their findings to the class and discuss what they discovered along the way.

Teams should be sure to cite all resources used. Some resources that may be helpful to the students include the following.

- **Blank map of USA (http://tinyurl.com/obcmptm):** There are many free sites available to choose the kind of blank map of the United States you would like to use. This site has the capitals marked.

- **MapQuest (mapquest.com):** This free site will help students find the shortest route from one point to another. They type in the address of their starting point, as well as their ending point. They also have the capability of finding alternate routes by moving the route marker around. This site does have ads.

- **Hotels (www.hotels.com):** This free site will help students find the cheapest hotel for any city they decide to stop in for the night. Students type in the city and state or point of interest location. Students can choose the type of hotel they want. This site does have ads.

- **Gas Prices (www.gasbuddy.com):** This free site will help students find the price of gas for any state in the United States. Simply put in the starting and ending points to generate a list of gas stations and prices. This site does have ads.

This lesson covers the **MP5** standard. Even though students are not creating stories or poems, they are taking notes, gathering relevant information from digital sources, citing sources, categorizing information, and creating explanations and justifications for travel across the country. They must also explain using the appropriate math vocabulary for this lesson. Therefore, this activity satisfies **SL.4.5** as well as **W.4.8**. Also satisfied with this activity is **W.4.6**, as students must find a way to produce and publish their mathematical thinking, reasoning, and problem solving for this task. When students present to the class, **W.4.7** and **SL.4.2** will be satisfied, as they need to interpret and paraphrase the information they are presenting orally and explain how the information being presented contributes to the understanding and justification that their team should finish first (especially so all other teams agree with their thinking and rationalizations).

A Final Note

It is clear that as students progress through the elementary grades, they are establishing their baseline of proficiency in technology. This will definitely enhance their experiences with technology in the upper grades, as well as satisfy the CCSS performance standards at the 3–5 level. We hope that you found the resources and lesson ideas presented in this chapter useful and that they are easy to adapt to your class.

You will find more resources online at **our website (http://tinyurl.com/oexfhcv)**, which may be helpful to you as you look to differentiate your instruction. Visit our site for updated information about this book. To learn more about meeting technology standards found within the CCSS in other grades, look for our three additional titles in this collection.

Chapter 10

Practical Ideas for Fifth Grade

We realize that you will want to focus on your particular grade or subject when you are planning your lessons and implementing CCSS, so we have organized the Practical Ideas chapters by grade level, then subject. Each grade starts with an overview followed by ELA technology standards with accompanying apps, software, and websites that you can use to help your students succeed with that standard. We then continue with the math standard for the grade level, also with accompanying resources. Finally, we have included some sample lessons for each grade level in various subject areas. Although we intend for you to seek your specific grade and subject to help you implement CCSS for your students, please do not disregard other sections of this chapter. To see grades other than 3–5, look for our three additional titles in this series, as they could provide information to help you differentiate for students at all levels of your class.

Fifth graders are expected to use technology to enhance their literacy skills. The emphasis here is to find information that is needed quickly and efficiently take notes, and document sources. They will need to take this information and publish their writing in a variety of ways, using tools such as digital dictionaries and the-sauruses. Reading texts is also emphasized. Finally, students will have to be quite proficient keyboardists by fifth grade. Technology should also be used to practice math skills, because students will need to use digital math tools available through software programs, apps, or websites. We have pulled out the fifth grade standards that include technology for you, and listed them in this chapter. We also offer ideas and suggestions on which technologies to use and how to teach with them.

Reading Resources

Microsoft PowerPoint (www.office.com) is often the presentation tool of choice—even with students—when using technology to produce and publish writing in a collaborative way. While this is still a great program, other presentation tools have emerged. Apple offers **Keynote (www.apple.com/mac/keynote)** as part of its software package. Its features are similar to PowerPoint. Another program that has emerged is **Google Slides (www.google.com/slides/about/)**. It is aimed toward business presentations; however, it is free and web-based. Google Slides makes it easy to share a project that multiple users can work on at once, which makes this an especially good program to use when interacting and collaborating remotely. You can also add audio recordings to your slides as well as visual displays such as pictures and short video clips. Having students create multimedia presentations and present them allows the class to analyze how visual and multimedia elements of the presentation contribute to the meaning, tone, or beauty of a text.

Reading Information

RL.5.7	READING LITERACY

Analyze how visual and **multimedia** elements contribute to the meaning, tone, or beauty of a text (e.g., graphic novel, **multimedia presentation** of fiction, folktale, myth, poem).

THE CCSS STANDARDS FOR READING are designed to help ensure that students gain adequate exposure to a range of texts and tasks. Rigor is also infused through the requirement that students read increasingly complex texts through the grades and make connections between text and visual or oral presentations.

SOFTWARE AND WEBSITES TO CREATE SLIDESHOWS

There are many ways that students can make visual and/or oral presentations from a piece of fiction, a folktale, myth, or poem. Using programs that allow students to illustrate as well as type improves the visual presentation of the text. Following are some examples of these programs.

- **Kid Pix (www.kidpix.com):** This software is not free, but students can use it to publish collaborative writing that uses pictures and text. There is a new version that features more animation called **Kid Pix 3D**.

- **Wixie (wixie.com) and Pixie (www.tech4learning.com/pixie):** This software for purchase uses multimedia, pictures, sound video, and text to create presentations and stories stored on the cloud for mobile access. The apps are free, but there is an online version for schools with more features that has educational pricing.

- **Smilebox (www.smilebox.com):** This is a free program linked to the website to create slideshows, invitations, greetings, collages, scrapbooks and photo albums right on your computer. Don't miss applying for the free Teacher's Toolbox!

- **Stupeflix (https://studio.stupeflix.com/en/):** Make free movies using your photos and videos for up to 20 minutes. It's very easy, and super fun!

All of these programs allow students to type in text and create their own illustrations. They also allow students to pick backgrounds from templates and to import pictures. They all put the presentations to be exported and viewed in a slideshow format, or they can be printed out as a storybook. Some even allow you to save them as ebooks. Smilebox or Stupeflix are free sites that allow you to make decorative slideshows.

ANIMATION APPS

The following resources are not easy to use with stories in paragraph form. However, you can use your voice to speak the text, and photos can be used to illustrate in an animated format. These apps allow students to create shorter versions of their stories in an animated way.

- **Puppet Pals (http://tinyurl.com/qbgaks2):** This app allows students to create a puppet production using familiar characters to tell or retell a story. It is free, but for $2.99, you can get all the add-ons.

- **iFunFace (www.ifunface.com):** Students can create a read-aloud to show how the main idea and details flow by using a photo and audio recording to create an animation. It helps students visualize how to support details that branch off from the main ideas and how they all flow together. App is free but can be upgraded for $1.99.

- **Blabberize (www.blabberize.com):** You can use your voice to speak the text, and photos can be used to illustrate in an animated format. Free.

- **Voki (www.voki.com):** Your voice speaks the text, and photos can be used to illustrate in an animated format. It is free, but there are ads.

- **Fotobabble (www.fotobabble.com):** You can use your voice to speak the text, and photos can be used to illustrate. Free.

Fifth grade students need to understand that although they can find information on any topic on the internet, finding the information that they need in a timely manner is not always easy. Learning which tool to use is important, as is understanding which sources are credible. Students can post a question on the search engine, and then sift through all of the sites, first reading the title of the link and then, if that is appropriate, the short summary. If after glancing through the web page they find it is not a site they are looking for (not the right information, or not a credible source), they can hit the back button and try again. Sometimes knowing exactly which site to use is helpful. For example, if they are looking for a definition, they should use an online dictionary such as **Webster's (www merriam-webster.com)**. A news site such as **Time for Kids (www.timeforkids.com)** could be used to find an answer to a current event, as could a local newspaper site like **Newsela (https:// e.newsela.com)**. **Weather.com (weather.com)** is a good place to go to see what the weather is like. Bookmarking sites that are popular for fifth grade can help students find answers to their questions quickly.

Doing an activity such as giving the class a sample question/problem and researching the answer together is a good way to get students started. They could then be given more sample questions with answers to be found with a partner. Then the answers could be gone over with the class as a group to discuss how everyone found them.

Writing Resources

Producing and publishing writing is not limited to slide show presentations, although **Google Docs (www.google.com/docs/about/)** is a great one to use as it makes collaboration easy, especially from home. There are many websites out there that allow you to publish student writing. Blogging websites such as **Edmodo (www.edmodo.com), KidBlog (www.kidblog.org)**, and **WikiSpaces (www.wikispaces.com)** are other places to share student writing in a safe, protected environment and another good way to interact and collaborate with others. These sites allow teachers to set themselves up as administrators and add students to different groups. All of the students' writing is kept secure in these groups.

Writing

THE COMMON CORE STANDARDS FOR K-5 writing offer a focus for instruction each year to help ensure that students gain adequate mastery of a range of skills and applications. Each year in their writing, students should demonstrate increasing sophistication in all aspects of language use, from vocabulary and syntax to the development and organization of ideas, and they should address increasingly demanding content and sources. Students advancing through the grades are expected to meet each year's grade-specific standards and retain or further develop skills and understandings mastered in preceding grades.

W.5.2	WRITING

Introduce a topic clearly, provide a general observation and focus, and group related information logically; include formatting (e.g., headings), illustrations, and **multimedia** when useful to aiding comprehension.

W.5.6	WRITING

With some guidance and support from adults, **use technology, including the Internet**, to produce and publish writing as well as to interact and collaborate with others; demonstrate sufficient command of **keyboarding skills** to type a minimum of two pages in a single sitting.

WEBSITES TO PUBLISH WRITING

You can give students assignments asking for short answers where everyone can respond in a blog format, or you can ask them to write longer assignments on their own that they work on as a document, then submit privately to you or post on a website to share. Using blogging programs, as well as other publishing tools, aids in comprehension, which satisfies standard **W.5.2** as well as **W.5.6**.

There are also websites that ask students to submit their work for possible publication on their site. Following are publishing websites to explore.

- **Scholastic Publishing: (http://tinyurl.com/plwnn6f):** This is a free website where teachers can submit student writing for publishing.

- **PBS Kids Writing (www.pbskids.org/writerscontest):** This free site asks for student writing and serves as a nice incentive to get students to do their best writing.

- **Lulu (www.lulu.com) and Lulu Jr (www.lulujr.com):** These sites allow you to create real books and publish them online. Parents can purchase the books as a keepsake. The site is free to use, but publishing them from Lulu Jr. is $19.

- **TikaTok (www.tikatok.com):** This is another site that allows students to write, create, and publish stories as ebooks or hardcover books. **TikaTok Story Spark** is an app that you can purchase for $3. Classroom price for TikaTok starts at $19/year.

- **Cast UDL Book Builder: (http://bookbuilder.cast.org):** This is a free site that lets you publish your ebook and see what others have published.

- **Poetry Idea Engine from Scholastic (http://tinyurl.com/2cuowf):** The site allows you to use templates to make different forms of poetry, another great way technology gets kids writing. Better still, it is free!

KEYBOARDING SOFTWARE

By fifth grade, students are expected to be able to type two pages in one sitting. There are plenty of keyboarding programs that you can buy. For example:

- **Mavis Beacon Keyboarding Kidz: (http://tinyurl.com/254v9on)** Set your own words-per-minute goals, see what keys you need to practice, and see what keys you know well. Play games to practice what you've learned and to improve your speed and accuracy to become a typing pro. ($19.99)

- **Type to Learn (http://ttl4.sunburst.com):** This typing program, for Grades K–12, emphasizes both accuracy and words-per-minute speed and provides each student with individualized remediation and goals for success. Consult the website for various pricing options and to request a quote.

- **Typing Training (www.typingtraining.com):** This web-based program with apps (for Grades 3–12) allows access from any computer or handheld device. Animated coaches are available with a customizable curriculum. Students can play games or choose from more than 2,500 unique exercises while tracking progress with detailed reports and graphs. Consult the website for various options and to request a quote.

KEYBOARDING WEBSITES

Paying for a good typing program is worth the expense. Quality programs keep track of student progress as well as their levels, teach the necessary skills, and allow students to access from home. If you can't buy a program, there are many free sites which offer some instruction and lots of games.

- **Dance Mat Typing (bbc.co.uk/guides/z3c6tfr):** This free website by BBC Schools teaches typing in an easy format.

- **TypingWeb (www.typing.com):** This site does have ads, but it keeps track of student progress with typing skills and allows reports. Free.

- **TypeRacer (www.play.typeracer.com):** Free website where you can race opponents by typing words in paragraph form. This website is for experienced typists to bone up on accuracy and typing speed. There are ads.

Some districts have students go to the computer labs where they practice keyboarding at given times, others fit it in where they can in the classroom and others have students practice and learn at home. We have found that the best way is to combine all three. Students benefit from formal keyboarding instruction, then they need to practice both in the classroom and at home. When students are working at the computers in your classroom, they need repeated reminders to keep up good techniques such as sitting up straight, keeping hands in home row, wrists slightly curved, and moving the fingers instead of the hands.

Writing Research

W.5.8	WRITING RESEARCH

Recall relevant information from experiences or gather relevant information from print and **digital sources**; summarize or paraphrase information in notes and finished work, and provide a list of sources.

BY THE TIME STUDENTS ARE IN FIFTH GRADE, they should be able to search the internet to gather the information that they need on a given topic. Your class will need guidance, of course, so lessons on internet searching are critical, as well as lessons on media literacy. (Media literacy is especially crucial, because students now need to be able to critique a website before using it—anyone can put up a webpage.) As stated by the **W.5.8** standard, students will also need to be able to take notes off these sites and summarize or paraphrase information as well as provide a list of sources. We discuss these techniques in the following paragraphs.

Although students are sufficiently net-savvy these days, they still need assistance with the basics of searching. Different search engines work in different ways, and each will give you different information. Your students need to know how to use multiple engines.

Smart searching will help avoid a lot of wasted time. Teaching students to analyze search results will definitely help them find better information and to think more critically about any information they find on the internet.

- Choose your search terms carefully. Be precise about what you are looking for, though you should use phrases and not full sentences.

- Adding more words can narrow a search. Use Boolean searches to narrow your topic with quotation marks. There's a big difference between "gopher" and "Habitats of gophers in North America."

- Use synonyms! If students can't find what they're looking for, have them try keywords that mean the same thing or are related.

- Type "site." Typing site: (with the colon) after your keyword and before a URL will tell Google to search within a specific website.

- Add a minus sign. Adding a minus sign (a hyphen) immediately before any word, with no space in between, indicates that you don't want that word to appear in your search results. For example, "Saturn -cars" will give you information about the planet, not the automobile.

KID-FRIENDLY SEARCH ENGINES

Browsing safe content is the most important reason for using search engines made specifically for kids. You may need to allow students to begin using adult search engines (such as Google, Yahoo, or Ask) in fifth grade to find more information than may be located in search engines for kids; however, it is always best for them to use kid-safe search engines when possible.

There is, of course, no guarantee that every search will be kid-safe. However, the search engines listed here are still your best bet.

- **Kids Click (www.kidsclick.org):** A web search site designed for kids by librarians with kid-friendly results. This site is free and for Grades 2-5.

- **Google for Kids (www.safesearchkids.com):** Google for Kids Safe Search Kids is a custom search engine using Google's Safe Search features with additional filtering to block more potentially harmful material than if you simply use Google. It is fun, colorful, and easy for students to use.

- **Google Kid Search (www.kidzsearch.com):** This is another safe search engine powered by Google for Grades K–8. However, please be aware there are ads on this site.

- **Yahoo for Kids (http://tinyurl.com/nqn4p39):** Yahooligans is a safe search engine for students picked by editors at Yahoo.

- **Ask Kids (www.ask.com):** This is a free, filtered search engine for Grades K–6.

Tried and true methods for taking notes and paraphrasing and summarizing information from books can still be used to gather information and take notes on websites. Teaching students to use data sheets, note cards, and KWL (Know, What, Learn) techniques still works; however, there are now ways that technology can help and sometimes make it easier. Apps such as **Evernote (www.evernote.com)** are a great way to take notes, as well as using a word processor program. Evernote is a very productive app to use. It allows you to import a worksheet, document, or picture, including a snapshot of a webpage. The **Kentucky Virtual Library (http://tinyurl.com/ptnwz4)** is a helpful website to use as a resource for some of these techniques. Students can then annotate their information using tools that they would use with interactive whiteboard software. Whiteboards let them highlight words, cut and paste, and add sticky notes. The sticky notes are especially useful to summarize or paraphrase students' notes. This website also allows students to use voice recognition. They can then send their annotated sheet to someone else (including the teacher).

Modeling is of course essential when you are teaching your students how to glean information from a website. Your interactive whiteboard is a perfect tool to use during your modeling lesson. Don't have an interactive whiteboard? Use **RealtimeBoard (www.realtimeboard.com).** It's a free website that allows you to turn an ordinary whiteboard into an interactive one. All you need is a computer and a projector! Using the many tools an interactive whiteboard and software have to offer will really help teach your students how to navigate through information posted on the internet.

MIND-MAPPING APPS AND WEBSITES

Using mind-mapping tools when gathering information will help your students organize their research. **Inspiration (www.inspiration.com)** is a wonderful software program that has been used for mind-mapping for many years. There are also some free sites out there that you can use, such as the following.

- **Bubbl.us (bubbl.us):** This is a free (with limited use) mind-mapping website for Grades K–12. It can be shared by multiple students at a time and comes with an accompanying app. For more options, purchase a package for $6/month or $59/year. Both come with a 30-day free trial. Site licensing is available. Contact the company for specifics.

- **Mindmeister (www.mindmeister.com/education):** This is a free, basic, mind-mapping website for Grades 2–12. Upgrades are available ($18/month for a single user; $30 per user for 6 months.) Educational pricing is available for schools and universities ($6 per user for 6 months). All of the upgrades have a free trial period.

- **FreeMind (http://tinyurl.com/5qrd5):** This is a free mind-mapping tool for Grades 2–12. However, FreeMind is written in Java and will run on almost any system with a Java runtime environment. Options for a basic or maximum install are available.

- **ClassTools (www.classtools.net):** Create graphs and charts, and use lots of other good classroom tools such as a QR code generator or timeline, with this free website.

Of course, word documents such as those that come with **Microsoft Office (www.office.com)**, **Pages (www.apple.com/mac/pages)**, or **Google Docs (www.google.com/docs/about)** can also be used. Some teachers also make digital templates to help students find specific information and organize their notes, with spaces to summarize or paraphrase.

Fifth graders will also need to provide a list of sources. Of course, making your own template for sources and having the students fill it in using a word processing program is an option; however, there are websites such as **EasyBib (www.easybib.com)**, that students can use to generate citations in MLA, APA, and Chicago formats easily. EasyBib is a free website and app for ages 5–12. Simply copy and paste or scan a book's barcode to generate its citation. Students can also cite a list of sources on their own by including URL, publisher or author, topic/title, and date website was published. If the date published is not available, then they should note the date retrieved from the internet.

Media Literacy Resources

Your class also needs to be aware that links come up in searches and some of them have strings attached — not to the research topic, but to advertisers. This should be a part of your media literacy lesson. Students can waste a lot of time if they don't realize what it is they are looking for. Students also need to know that anyone can put up a website, and they need to know how to tell whether a website is credible. Determining whether a site is a .com (stands for company), .gov (a government site), or .org (a nonprofit organization such as a school) is the first step. Then students need to be able to identify who the author of the site is (this will usually be posted at the beginning or the end), who they are affiliated with, or what is the author's background or expertise on the topic. Your students will also need to know that advertisers abound, and students will need to be careful what they click on. The class needs to be taught what to do if they go to an inappropriate site (such as hitting the back button immediately and letting a teacher know) The website **Joe Cool/Joe Fool (http://tinyurl.com/pojhuuw)** is a good site to use. It provides online media literacy lessons complete with quizzes.

Speaking and Listening

SL.5.2	SPEAKING AND LISTENING

Summarize a written text read aloud or information presented in **diverse media and formats**, including visually, quantitatively, and orally.

SL.5.5	SPEAKING AND LISTENING

Include **multimedia** components (e.g., graphics, sound) and **visual displays** in presentations when appropriate to enhance the development of main ideas or themes.

THERE ARE MANY DIVERSE MEDIA formats that will now read aloud to students. Books read on CD or some e-books are good sources to use. Sites such as **Follett Shelf (http://tinyurl.com/oux56og)** and **TumbleBooks (www.tumblebooks. com)** (must be purchased) give you access to multiple e-book collections that include fiction as well as nonfiction. You can also check out many e-books at your local library or purchase them from booksellers like Amazon or Barnes & Noble (especially if you have e-readers). There are also some free e-books available. **Project Gutenberg (http://gutenberg.org/)**, **FreeReadFeed (www.freereadfeed.com)**, or **FreeBookSifter (www.freebooksifter.com)**, are possibilities. There are adult titles on these sites, too, so choose carefully. Of course, sites that you pay for give you a much better selection. Using e-books or a website with your interactive whiteboard (or free whiteboard sites) allows interaction when modeling or for student engagement. Informational text works especially well with this standard; however, fictional pieces can also be used.

INTERACTIVE APPS AND WEBSITES

After listening to the text read aloud, students can use different media formats to summarize what they heard. Because students are summarizing and keeping it short, they can use these fun, interactive apps.

- **iFunFace (www.ifunface.com):** Students can create a read-aloud to show how the main idea and details flow by using a photo and audio recording to create an animation. It helps students visualize how to support details that branch off from the main ideas and how they all flow together. The app is free but can be upgraded for $1.99.

- **Comic Life (http://tinyurl.com/oj5o2qd):** This tool can be purchased as software or as an app. Make a comic from your own images with fonts, templates, panels, balloons, captions, and lettering art.

- **ToonDoo (www.toondoo.com):** Create your own comics to upload online, or create a comic storybook. The app is free; however, you can also purchase printable images or ToonDooSpaces.

- **iMovie (www.apple.com/ios/imovie):** This $4.99 app, which is also available as a program, has many uses in the classroom to create full edited videos or short 1-minute trailers. The trailers can be useful for recounting and presenting ideas to others.

- **Animoto (www.animoto.com):** This website allows you to turn your photos and music into stunning video slideshows. Educational use is free for unlimited videos of 20 minutes.

- **Puppet Pals (http://tinyurl.com/qbgaks2):** This app allows students to create a puppet production using familiar characters to tell or retell a story. It is free, but for $2.99 you can get all the add-ons.

MIND-MAPPING SOFTWARE, WEBSITES, AND APPS

Working with the teacher or on their own, students need to understand the development of the main idea or themes of a text. Mind-mapping programs are a good place to start to organize text with main ideas. Students can visually see how the supporting details branch off from the main idea and how they all flow together. Some examples of these programs follow.

- **Inspiration (http://tinyurl.com/ygharef):** This is a mind-mapping software program that helps student organize their writing. It can be especially helpful for students who are learning to create paragraphs and organize big ideas into smaller parts. Cost is $40 to $640. The web-based version is called

Webspiration (http://tinyurl.com/bmop3nh) and costs $6/month.

- **Popplet (www.popplet.com):** A wonderful online organizational tool for students' writing. A free app called **Popplet Lite** is also available. It is easy to use, and students can import pictures and text to create web maps.

- **Bubbl.us (https://bubbl.us):** This is a free (with limited use) mind-mapping website for Grades K–12. It can be shared by multiple students at a time and comes with an app. For more options, purchase a package for $6/month or $59/year. Both come with a 30-day free trial. Site licensing is available. Contact the company for specifics.

- **Mindmeister (www.mindmeister.com/education):** This is a free, basic, mind-mapping website for Grades 2–12. Upgrades are available ($18/month for a single user; $30 per user for 6 months). Educational pricing is available for schools and universities ($6 per user for 6 months). All of the upgrades have a free trial period.

- **FreeMind (http://tinyurl.com/5qrd5):** This is a free mind-mapping tool for Grades 2–12. However, FreeMind is written in Java and will run on almost any system with a Java runtime environment. Options for a basic or maximum install are available.

APPS AND WEBSITES USING ANIMATION

Students can include multimedia components and visual displays when presenting their main ideas or themes by taking their mind maps and creating a "read aloud" using an app that allows them to have a character recite their presentation. Of course, PowerPoint, Google Slides or Keynote also work well when presenting and including multimedia components and visual displays. Following are some apps and websites that use visuals as well as sound.

- **iFunFace (www.ifunface.com):** Students can create a read-aloud to show how the main idea and details flow by using a photo and audio recording to create an animation. It helps students visualize how to support details that branch off from the main ideas and how they all flow together. The app is free but can be upgraded for $1.99.

- **Puppet Pals (http://tinyurl.com/qbgaks2):** This app allows students to create a puppet production using familiar characters to tell or retell a story. It is free, but for $2.99, you can get all the add-ons.

- **Blabberize (www.blabberize.com):** You can use your voice to speak the text, and photos can be used to illustrate in an animated format. Free.

- **Voki (www.voki.com):** You can use your voice to speak the text and photos can be used to illustrate in an animated format. It is free, but there are ads.

- **Fotobabble (www.fotobabble.com):** You can use your voice to speak the text, and photos can be used to illustrate. Free.

APPS AND WEBSITES FOR PRESENTATIONS

Following are resources that students can use to share work and create presentations.

- **Prezi (www.prezi.com):** You can sign up for a free educational account, and your students can create and share presentations online. Prezi has mind-mapping, zoom, and motion and can import files. Presentations can be downloaded. A Prezi viewer app is available.

- **Wixie (www.wixie.com) and Pixie (www.tech4learning.com/pixie):** This software for purchase uses multimedia, pictures, sound video, and text to create presentations and stories stored in the cloud for mobile access. The apps are free, but there is an online version for schools with more features that has educational pricing.

- **WebQuests (www.webquest.org):** These are excellent tools to use for presentations. WebQuest is a website that allows students to follow an already-created, project-based lesson where information is found solely on the internet. Students can also create their own WebQuest if a website building program or a website like **Kafafa (www.kafafa.com/kafafa)** is available. WebQuest.org is the original and most popular site; however, if you search the internet, you will find more sites that you can use.

Language Resources

Merriam-Webster (www.merriam-webster.com) is still the most commonly used digital dictionary and thesaurus. They also offer a kid-friendly version of this dictionary called **Word Central (www.wordcentral.com)**. This resource includes the pronunciation of the word as well as its definition. The original Merriam-Webster site has this as well, and includes multiple definitions. **Kids.Wordsmyth (www./kids. wordsmyth.net/we)** and **WordSmyth (www.wordsmyth.net)** are good fifth grade options. The kids' version includes pronunciation (as does the adults') and shows how words are used as a part of speech with examples and pictures if applicable.

Little Explorers (http://tinyurl.com/2swjc) is another good option for a dictionary and thesauruses, and it includes a glossary maker. You can sign up for an ad-free version, which will not cost your school. **Thesaurus.com (www.thesaurus.com)** is a great thesaurus site. While digital dictionaries and thesauruses are not updated as often as encyclopedias, they are still very convenient to use and are kept current. These sites should be bookmarked or put on your website for easy access. The more students use them, the more comfortable they will become. You should offer lessons and activities to learn and practice the necessary skills with an online dictionary, just as you would when using hard-copy dictionaries, glossaries, and thesauruses.

Language

> **L.5.4c** | LANGUAGE
>
> Consult reference materials (e.g., dictionaries, glossaries, thesauruses), both print and **digital**, to find the pronunciation and determine or clarify the precise meaning of key words and phrases.

A LESSON PLAN IDEA WHEN USING electronic dictionaries is to look up difficult vocabulary words in a piece of informational text. You could give students a website (preferably on a standards topic from literacy or science) and ask them to write down all of the words they don't know. They can use an electronic dictionary to find the definitions to these words. They then reread the passage, and, with luck, will come away with a better understanding of its content.

Using the app or website **Trading Cards (http://tinyurl.com/8lqftek)** is a great way to document vocabulary words by adding their definitions, a picture, and recordings of pronunciations. You can also use Trading Cards as part of a fun activity that uses an online thesaurus. Simply give a student a word on a trading card, and then ask them to make as many trading cards as they can of synonyms and antonyms of that word. They can print these out and trade them with others or make them into a digital book.

Math Resources

THERE ARE TWO MAIN SETS OF BENCHMARKS–processes and practices–for the Common Core Math standards. First, you have the math targets, written similarly to ELA (Counting and Cardinality; Operations & Algebraic Thinking; Number & Operation in Base Ten; Measurement & Data; and Geometry). While you work with students on mathematical processes like base ten and fractions in fifth grade, you need to teach your students how to apply the Standards for Mathematical Practices, such as problem solving and precision, to those processes. One practice, the only one that includes technology, is mathematical practice 5, "Use appropriate tools strategically."

MP5	MATH
Use appropriate **tools** strategically.	

Following is the explanation CCSS provides for **MP5**. As this is the standard explanation for Grades K–12, it does include references to higher grades.

> Mathematically proficient students consider the available tools when solving a mathematical problem. These tools might include pencil and paper, concrete models, a ruler, a protractor, **a calculator, a spreadsheet, a computer algebra system, a statistical package, or dynamic geometry software**. Proficient students are sufficiently familiar with tools appropriate for their grade or course to make sound decisions about when each of these tools might be helpful, recognizing both the insight to be gained and their limitations. For example, mathematically proficient high school students analyze graphs of functions and solutions generated using a **graphing calculator**. They detect possible errors by strategically using estimation and other mathematical knowledge. When making mathematical models, they know that technology can enable them to visualize the results of varying assumptions, explore consequences, and compare predictions with data. Mathematically proficient students at various grade levels are able to identify relevant external mathematical resources, such as **digital content located on a website**, and use them to pose or solve problems. They are able to use **technological tools** to explore and deepen their understanding of concepts.

Because this description did not give examples for all grades, we have provided a list of appropriate apps, websites, software, and included lessons that will help translate this standard for fifth grade.

Currently, this is the only fifth grade math standard that involves technology. Since using any kind of technology to have students practice math can grab their attention, help long-term learning, and make math fun, technology is a math tool that students should use as much as possible. There are many math programs, websites, and apps out there, which allows students to explore and deepen their understanding of math concepts. The best of them have students learning in creative ways and are not just electronic worksheets. They automatically adapt to the students' skill levels, and they give you the data you need to know where students are in their learning and what they need to effectively continue. Of course, these usually do not come free. Following are many good math resources. Some are free, some are not. Unfortunately, the free resources, many with ads, are often less interesting to your students and not as well organized. They don't give you the feedback you need. It is up to you to make the decision about what is best for your circumstances and budget.

MATH WEBSITES

Following are some tools you can use to help students meet the fifth grade math standards.

- **ScootPad (www.scootpad.com):** This is a web-based math site that is totally customizable for individual students. It adapts to the student and keeps the teacher in the loop with multiple reports. It is completely aligned to the CCSS. The price for a class varies from $5 to $20/month.

- **DreamBox Learning Math (www.dreambox.com):** This individualized, adaptive game-based math tool keeps students coming back for more. It is available online or as an app. Price is $12.95/month (home) or $25/month (school), less if packaged.

- **IXL (www.ixl.com/math):** This online site features adaptive, individualized math through gameplay. It gives students immediate feedback and covers many skills, despite its emphasis on drills. Levels range from pre-kindergarten to eighth grade. Class price is $199/year.

- **Starfall (www.starfall.com):** This free website has a few clever activities for early literacy and math exploration, but the pay site, **More.Starfall**, has a full range of activities. Cost is $70 to $270/year.

- **XtraMath (www.xtramath.org):** This is a great site for practicing math facts. It keeps track of student progress, it's easy to pick what you want students to work on, and it's easy for students to use independently. And it's free!

- **PrimaryGames (www.primarygames.com/math.php), Coolmath-Games (Cool-math-Games.com), SoftSchools (SoftSchools.com),** and **Sheppard Software (http://tinyurl.com/ccrxoa)** are several sites that have free math games covering all math topics at each grade level. However, they have ads, are not able to keep track of a student's success rates, and are not generally self-adaptive to skill level.

- **Khan Academy (www.khanacademy.org):** This free website has every math application you can think of and has short video tutorials on how to solve them.

- **AdaptedMind (http://tinyurl.com/997geeg):** This free website is a good practice tool for all sorts of fifth grade math problems.

- **Thinking Blocks (http://tinyurl.com/3c6eoa):** The site provides manipulatives with blocks so you can model, solve word problems, and practice with fractions. It is available as a free app.

MATH APPS

There are many math apps available. The following recommendations are ideal for fifth grade students.

- **Explain Everything (www.explaineverything.com):** This $2.99 app uses text, video, pictures, and voice to present whatever you ask students to create.

- **Math Blaster HyperBlast (http://tinyurl.com/q3ff7vg):** The classic game many teachers used when they were students is now updated. Cost is $0.99 to $1.99.

- **Geoboard (http://tinyurl.com/kzyxjv7):** This app is the digital recreation of a geoboard. The app is simple to use, and the geometry activities are open-ended and endless. The app is free.

- **Swipea Tangram Puzzles for Kids (http://tinyurl.com/nsnoazj):** This is a digital version of tangrams where students can manipulate, flip, and rotate shapes to create different pictures. App is free. Full upgrade is $0.99.

- **The Geometer's Sketchpad (www.keycurriculum.com):** Students can manipulate dynamic models of fractions, number lines, and geometric patterns. Middle school students can build their readiness for algebra by exploring ratio and proportion, rate of change, and functional relationships through multiple representations. More advanced students can use **Sketchpad Explorer** to construct and transform geometric shapes and functions, from linear to trigonometric. Pricing for the software version is determined by the number of computers used. For example, cost is $15 for 100+ computers versus $70 for 1 to 4 computers.

GRAPHING SOFTWARE AND WEBSITES

As stated in the standard, "Mathematically proficient students consider the available tools when solving a mathematical problem. These tools might include a calculator, a spreadsheet, a computer algebra system, a statistical package, or dynamic geometry software. Proficient students are sufficiently familiar with tools appropriate for their grade or course to make sound decisions about when each of these tools might be helpful, recognizing both the insight to be gained and their limitations."

There are many sites that allow you to use math tools such as a graphing calculator. Another option is to use software that comes with your whiteboard. These have all sorts of built-in mathematical tools such as protractors, rulers, and grids. You can use your interactive whiteboard for many of these functions. Don't have an interactive whiteboard? Use **RealtimeBoard (www.realtimeboard.com)**! It's a free website that allows you to turn an ordinary whiteboard into an interactive one. All you need is a computer and a projector! Following are some good programs and sites to use when graphing.

- **SoftSchools (www.softschools.com):** This is one of several sites that have free math games that cover all math topics at each grade, including graphs However, they have ads, are not able to keep track of a student's success rate, and are not generally self-adaptive to students' skill levels. Free.

- **IXL (www.ixl.com/math):** This online site features adaptive individualized math through gameplay including problems involving data and graphs. This gives students immediate feedback and covers many skills, despite its emphasis on drills. Levels range from pre-kindergarten to eighth grade. Class price is $199/year.

- **The Graph Club 2.0 (http://bit.ly/1nmvNe6):** This program really helps students visualize how charts and graphs compare, and it's extremely easy to use. The program includes ready-made activities in all subject areas including rubrics and sample graphs. District purchasing and volume CDs are available. Contact a representative on the site for specific prices.

- **Gliffy (www.gliffy.com):** Create professional-quality flowcharts, wireframes, diagrams, and more. Free for limited use. Upgrades available for a fee.

- **Create-a-Graph (http://tinyurl.com/yoedjn):** Create bar, line, area, pie, and XY graphs with this free website. Easy to use, and you can print, save, or e-mail your completed graphs.

- **ClassTools (www.classtools.net):** Students can create graphs and charts with the tools on this free site. It has many other useful classroom tools, such as a QR code generator and timeline.

In fifth grade, students are also expected to use a protractor to measure angles. They can use the app **Protractor 1st (www.skypaw.com/apps)**, which is part of the Multi Measures 2 app that includes a converter that can measure pairs of units. **Softpedia (www.softpedia.com)** is a site that allows you to download a protractor to use online. The site is free, but has ads. Using your interactive whiteboard protractor tool also works well.

Many studies in recent years have shown how math games can increase student learning. In addition, a survey (http://tinyurl.com/pqms3nj) released in late summer 2014 from the Games and Learning Publishing Council indicates that the use of digital games in the classroom is becoming more popular with teachers. According to the survey, 55% of teachers who responded have students play digital games in their classroom weekly.

With this in mind, pick a math unit of study. You may wish to first research this math topic and find videos to show as an introduction. Videos from **BrainPOP (www.brainpop.com)**, **Khan Academy (www.khanacademy.org)**, and **School Tube (www.schooltube.com)** are just a few good sources we have found. However, please be advised that you should view any video before showing it to the class. These activities are also a great way to set up guided math stations or learning centers. Problem-solving activities are also an effective way to differentiate if you happen to have some students who are moving through lessons faster than the rest of the class.

Literacy Lessons

Cross-curriculum planning is encouraged with the common core by using ELA standards in history, science, and technical subjects. Getting through all of the standards you need in fifth grade is very difficult in the time given. The key to planning with the CCSS is by teaching multiple standards in one lesson, when you can. We hope that the following list of a few sample lessons for fifth grade will inspire you to become an effective technology lesson planner.

SUMMARY WRITING

Several fifth grade colleagues have used the following activity when they want their students to show what they know for summary writing. Choose a nonfiction or current-event text for students to read. Our teachers like **Newsela Elementary (https://e.newsela.com)**. You may also switch things around and have your students choose their own article for this activity. When students finish reading, they need to begin brainstorming for their summaries. You can use any form of brainstorming writing technique that suits you. Our colleagues and their students have success with the jot dot technique.

Using the iMovie Trailer app, students make a movie trailer for their nonfiction summary, using pictures they find on the internet. Students must include titles, subtitles, and keywords to describe their article summary. Students also select music to fit the summary and import it into the iMovie Trailer. As students read, they should be encouraged to look up and determine the meaning of unfamiliar words. When they do this, standard **L.5.4c** will be satisfied. Using iMovie Trailer, picking pictures to illustrate their summaries, and the type of music chosen will satisfy standard **RL.5.7**, as students are taking responsibility for establishing the meaning and tone of their iMovie Trailer summary. Also satisfied with this activity are **W.5.2**, **W.5.6**, and **W.5.8**. Furthermore, **SL.5.2** and **SL.5.5** will be satisfied, as students are using iMovie Trailer as their multimedia presentation.

CULMINATING RAPS

Even though this next lesson was done during literacy time, you can use any subject and/or topic. This fifth grade class was studying metaphors and similes. As a culminating project, students wrote raps and performed them for the class.

- First, the class brainstormed 15 to 20 key words for metaphors and similes, with the teacher writing and displaying the words on the whiteboard.

- Working in pairs or groups of no more than four, students discussed and picked 8 to 10 of the keywords they felt were interesting and would work in their rap.

- Next, students took each keyword and found 8 to 10 rhymes.

- Then, using the keywords and rhymes, students wrote sentences. These sentences all related to the topic of metaphors and similes. Each keyword had at least four sentences, and students could choose their rhyming pattern (for example, AA BB or AB AB).

- Once students completed their writing, they moved on to finding the beat for their rap. Using **GarageBand (www.apple.com/mac/garageband/)** or any other app or software that promotes music creation, students rehearsed their raps (slowing the beat down or speeding it up if need be).

- Students could perform their raps "live" in front of the class. But, most chose to record themselves with their tablets (one tablet videoing the performance and the other playing their rap on GarageBand). Students then streamed the audio or video to show the class.

This engaging project satisfies a myriad of fifth grade standards, specifically **L.5.4c**, as students should be encouraged to be creative to find words that rhyme with their keywords and therefore should consult reference materials, such as dictionaries and thesauruses. **SL.5.2** and **SL.5.5** are also satisfied, as students are summarizing what they learned about metaphors and similes and presenting using diverse media, including sound. All of the fifth grade writing standards are also satisfied with this lesson—**W.5.2**, **W.5.8**, and especially **W.5.6**, as students will need guidance and support from adults as they work with others to produce their rap.

Social Studies and Science Lessons

The following sample lessons address CCSS ELA standards and teach content based on national standards in social studies and science.

SLAVERY ACTIVITY

During social studies, fifth grade students learn about the Civil War. As part of this unit, former fifth grade colleagues of ours brought in a study of slavery and did an integrated lesson with literacy and art. The first step is to find interactive text, websites, videos, art, music, etc., to share on your whiteboard. BrainPOP has a multitude of movies, ideas, and activities on this topic. After watching, listening, and discussing this period in our history, students work in pairs to find examples of songs, ballads, poems, and art that they are interested in. YouTube is a great source for songs, ballads, and spoken poems. As students search, they should be encouraged to look up and determine the meaning of unfamiliar words or phrases they encounter. When they do this, standard **L.5.4c** will be satisfied. Next, students choose their favorite song, ballad, or poem to write a parody. Teams may wish to write their rough draft using any document or presentation tool (PowerPoint, Keynote, etc.). Students will also make artwork (quilts, signs, drawings, etc.) to illustrate their song, ballad, or poem. This can be done using Google Draw, Microsoft Draw, or something similar. For students' final presentations, keeping in mind that they will be sharing with their classmates, students select which technology they will use to present their song/ballad/poem and artwork (iMovie Trailer, iMovie, Wixie, Explain Everything, GarageBand, etc.). Next, students present to the class by projecting (RealtimeBoard) their tablet onto the interactive whiteboard. Students listen carefully to each presentation (taking notes using Evernote) and ask questions at the end. Students giving the presentation must be able to answer questions quickly and efficiently. Students research and understand the meaning, tone, and beauty of the songs, ballads, and poems of that time. This satisfies standards **RI.5.7**, **W.5.2**, **W.5.6**, and **W.5.8**. In addition, the presentation part of this activity satisfies **SL.5.2** and **SL.5.5**.

MYSTERY PLANETS

Because fifth graders across the country study the solar system, this great activity coincides with a science lesson on astronomy or space. Create a planet riddle using the Puppet Pals 2 app on a tablet. First, gather clues using BrainPOP and A Solar System Journey apps. Each student group provides clues for their "mystery" planet. Next, the group writes a "script" that includes the clues researched—for example: "My planet is the fifth planet from the Sun," or "This planet is the largest in the solar system. Who am I?" Next, students head to Puppet Pals 2 and create their riddle. When finished, students save their video as "Mystery Planet" (with the number given to their group). Upload the mystery planet videos to YouTube, and another fifth grade class will try to solve the riddles. The "guest" teacher will have the answers, so your students shouldn't reveal the name of the planet in their video! This engaging lesson satisfies **RI.5.5**, as students will get to know and use various text features to locate key facts or information in a text efficiently, specifically with their research. **RL.5.8** is also met with this activity. Working with and collaborating on their Puppet Pals 2 slide show would then satisfy **W.5.6**, as well as **SL.5.2**. Even though students are not creating a story or poem, they are creating clues for riddles. Therefore, this activity also satisfies **SL.5.5**.

Math Lessons

The following lesson samples satisfy standard MP5 in addition to several ELA standards.

SHAPE GEOMETRY

Teacher friends of ours use this math activity for a unit on geometry, which involves students creating and comparing two-dimensional and three-dimensional shapes. They also list specific attributes of each shape in their comparison. Students can be paired or work in small groups while using the computer program Geometer's

Sketchpad to create shapes from a teacher-made list. Students jot down attributes of each of the three-dimensional shapes, making sure they give proper number of sides, angles, and so on. Next, using the app Explain Everything, students create their two-dimensional shapes. Finally, students present their findings to the class by projecting their Geometer's Sketchpad and Explain Everything drawings. Students follow up with questions to the presenter, making sure they can distinguish between the two-dimensional and three-dimensional shapes presented. This intriguing and popular lesson covers **MP5** by using digital tools to enhance mathematical learning. Even though students are not creating stories or poems, they are creating explanations for their geometric shapes and must be able to explain them using the appropriate math attributes and other math vocabulary for this lesson. Therefore, this activity also satisfies **SL.5.5**. **W.5.6** is satisfied as well with this activity, as students are using the app Explain Everything to produce and publish their mathematical thinking, reasoning, and problem solving for this task.

3D PLANETS

The fifth grade students in our state study the planets (NSTA Standards). This lesson combines our very successful science lesson with the applied math fifth graders need to know, as well as a dose of reading, writing and speaking. Students break into eight or nine small groups (one for each planet) to create a 3D model of the planets (we used a Styrofoam circle and added modeling clay to get the precise size) and scale model of the solar system (lots of measurement and conversion.) The groups create a scale model of their planet and also where it fits into the solar system using the math standards **MP5**. Students also use their notes from videos they view, research they complete on the internet, trade books, and textbooks to create a presentation of their planet findings. Using iMovie Trailer, Prezi, Explain Everything, or any presentation app or program, students summarize their research, satisfying standard **RI.5.7**. Students draw on information from multiple print and digital sources, demonstrating the ability to locate an answer to a question quickly or to solve a problem efficiently. Also satisfied with this activity are **W.5.2** and **W.5.6**, as well as **W.5.8**. Furthermore, **SL.5.2** and **SL.5.5** will be satisfied, as students are using digital media such as iMovie for their presentation.

A Final Note

It is clear that as students progress through the elementary grades, they are establishing their baseline of proficiency in technology. This will definitely enhance their experiences with technology in the upper grades, as well as satisfy the CCSS performance standards at the 3–5 level. We hope that you found the resources and lesson ideas presented in this chapter useful and that they are easy to adapt to your class.

You will find more resources online at **our website (http://tinyurl.com/oexfhcv)**, which may be helpful to you as you look to differentiate your instruction. Visit our site for updated information about this book. To learn more about meeting technology standards found within the CCSS for other grades, look for our three additional titles in this collection.

References

DeWitt, P. (2013, July 7). *Take a risk...Flip your parent communication!* [Blog post]. Retrieved from http://blogs.edweek.org/edweek/finding_common_ground/2013/07/take_a_risk_flip_your_parent_communication.html

Edutopia (2007). What is successful technology integration? *Technology Integration Professional Development Guide.* Retrieved from http://www.edutopia.org/technology-integration-guide-description

Henderson. A., & Mapp, K. (2002). *A new wave of evidence: The impact of school, family, and community connections on student achievement* (Annual Synthesis 2002). Retrieved from Southwest Educational Development Laboratory website: http://www.sedl.org/connections/resources/evidence.pdf

LEAD Commission. (2012). *Parents' and teachers' attitudes and opinions on technology in education.* (National online survey, August 2012). Retrieved from LEAD Commission website: http://www.leadcommission.org/sites/default/files/LEAD Poll Deck.pdf

Meeuwse, K. (2013, April 11). *Using iPads to transform teaching and learning* [Blog post]. Retrieved from http://iteachwithipads.net/2013/04/11/using-ipads-to-transform-teaching-and-learning

National Governors Association Center for Best Practices & Council of Chief State School Officers. (2010). *Common Core State Standards*. Washington, DC: Authors.

New York University. (2007) *National Symposium on the Millennial Student*. Retrieved from http://www.nyu.edu/frn/publications/millennial.student/Millennial.index.html

Partnership for 21st Century Skills. (2004). *The partnership for 21st century skills-Framework for 21st century learning*. Retrieved from http://www.p21.org/about-us/p21-framework

Sammons, L. (2009). *Guided math a framework for mathematics instruction*. Huntington Beach: Shell Education.

Sammons, L. (2011, September 21). Guided math: a framework for math instruction. Retrieved June 25, 2015, from http://www.slideshare.net/ggierhart/guided-math-powerpointbytheauthorofguidedmath

Strategic Learning Programs. (n.d.). Retrieved from http://www.iste.org/lead/professional-services/strategic-learning-programs

Swanson, K. (2013, October 1). Tips for explaining common core to parents—*THE Journal*. Retrieved from https://thejournal.com/articles/2013/10/01/how-to-explain-common-core-to-parents.aspx http://thejournal.com/2013/10/01/how-to-explain-common-core-to-parents.aspx

Szybinski, D. (2007). From the Executive Director - *NETWORK: A Journal of Faculty Development*. Retrieved from http://tinyurl.com/pqwr7va

United States Congress. (2010) Section 1015c. Chapter 28: Higher education resources and student assistance. In *Title 20–Education* (2010 ed.). Retrieved from http://www.gpo.gov/fdsys/pkg/USCODE-2010-title20/html/USCODE-2010-title20-chap28.htm